The Test Match Career of
GEOFFREY
BOYCOTT

The Test Match Career of
GEOFFREY BOYCOTT

C.D. Clark

Foreword by David Frith
Photography by Patrick Eagar

SPELLMOUNT LTD
Tunbridge Wells · Kent

Being prepared in the same series:

Sir Donald Bradman
Walter Hammond
Jim Laker
Denis Compton

First published in the U.K. in 1986 by
SPELLMOUNT LTD
12 Dene Way, Speldhurst
Tunbridge Wells, Kent TN3 0NX
ISBN 0–946771–07–3

British Library Cataloguing in
Publication Data
Clark, Christopher
   The test match career of Geoffrey Boycott.
   1. Boycott, Geoff   2. Cricket player —
   Great Britain — Biography
   I. Title
   796.35'0924   GV915.B6/

Design by Words & Images, Speldhurst,
Tunbridge Wells, Kent
Typesetting by Metra Graphic,
Southborough, Tunbridge Wells, Kent
Printed in Great Britain by
Adlard & Son Ltd, Dorking, Surrey

Contents

Acknowledgements

List of illustrations

Foreword

1 A good start   13

2 Home and abroad   18

3 Fluctuating fortunes   28

4 Indian stunner, West Indies summer   39

5 Missed Tests and West Indies again   51

6 A glorious run of runs   61

7 Revenge at last on New Zealand   71

8 Towards the break   79

9 The greatest moment   86

10 A sudden change of heart   93

11 In the wake of strife   100

12 West Indies all the way   108

13 A record to take home – straightaway   116

14 An ignominious end   125

Statistics   129

Index   143

Acknowledgements

The Author would like to offer his sincere and grateful thanks to the numerous people who, at varying stages of the book, all combined to make the end-result possible. They were:

Guisborough County Library
Angela Cook, Yvonne Dawson, Carole Logan, Caroline Rogers and Ian Wilson.

Middlesbrough Central Reference Library
Andrea Barker, Larry Bruce, Tracey Coates, Anne Nichol, Moira Smith, Mrs J. Waites and Jackie Whittle.

Redcar Central Library
Jane Booth, Maggie Doyle, Ray Hyde and Ian Tansley.

Also, Roger Butterfield and Charlie Bell for their patient scrutinising of the manuscript; Neil Johnson and Derek Lodge, for supplying crucial statistics; and finally, but not least, Marion Prest, Christine Dales and Gill Cooke, whose typing was the most important task of all.

List of illustrations
All photographs by Patrick Eager

1 **1974** *Test Trial at Worcester. Geoff Boycott (Yorks), John Lever (Essex) is the bowler.*
2 **1977** *Third Test, England v Australia, Trent Bridge. Geoff Boycott batting during stand with Alan Knott.*
3 **1977** *Fourth Test, England v Australia, Headingley. Geoff Boycott reaches his 100th first class century with this on drive off Greg Chappell.*
4 **1977** *Fourth Test, England v Australia, Headingley. Geoff Boycott scores his 100th first class century.*
5 **1978** *Second Test, England v New Zealand, Trent Bridge. Geoff Boycott.*
6 **1978** *Second Test, England v New Zealand, Trent Bridge. Geoff Boycott.*
7 **1978** *Second Test, England v New Zealand, Trent Bridge. Geoff Boycott acknowledges applause on reaching century.*
8 **1978** *Third Test, England v New Zealand, Lord's. Geoff Boycott.*
9 **1979** *First Test, England v India, Edgbaston. Boycott reaches century.*
10 **1978** *Geoff Boycott v Hampshire, Southampton.*
11 **1979** *First Test, England v India at Edgbaston. Boycott batting during his 155.*
12 **1980** *Geoff Boycott before the Test v the West Indies, The Oval.*
13 **1980** *Second Test, England v West Indies, Lord's. Geoff Boycott bowling, Lloyd backs up and Willey is the fielder.*
14 **1980** *Centenary Test, England v Australia, Lord's. Boycott cuts Pascoe.*
15 **1981** *Geoff Boycott batting v Barbados, Bridgetown.*
16 **1980** *Fourth Test, England v the West Indies, The Oval. Bacchus inspects Boycott after he had been hit by Croft. In spite of wearing a crash helmet, he suffered a cut about the eye.*
17 **1981** *Fifth Test, England v Australia, Old Trafford. Geoff Boycott with a hairy intruder.*

Foreword

They say he's an enigma, but I'm not so sure. There is nothing greatly puzzling or unique about a man, in any walk of life, who pursues his aim to such fiercely determined lengths that he loses the sense of proportion. How many millionaires do you know who are 'normal', whether self-made or otherwise? Indeed, how many millionaires do you truly know? How many power-wielding politicians are renowned for the modesty and down-to-earth attitude? And what about the acting fraternity? How relaxed and balanced is your average thespian when off duty?

Geoff Boycott's problem, if one may presume to suggest that he has one, is that for twenty years his dedication to survival at the batting crease and to the accumulation of runs has been so intense as to be indistinguishable from a self-interest of the strangulating kind. It was apparent from the 1983 revolt, which took him from banishment not only back into the Yorkshire team but on to the county club committee, that there are several thousand awed Yorkshiremen, at least, who regard his prolific scoring as quite sufficient justification for believing in him. But those who had become disenchanted while playing alongside him did not view him from the same angle. The milieu of the millionaire, the politician or the actor is a long way removed from that of the cricketer, where humility and a certain generosity of spirit are not only advisable but expected – by some, demanded.

Geoff Boycott's dedication is legendary. It has also become blinding. Shutting out the Australians for hours on end is fine; indeed, sometimes bordering on the heroic. Boring a third-day midweek crowd at Northampton or Gloucester with deliberate batting parsimony may be understood only by dozing and easily-satisfied escapees from the traumas of the outside world or by those with the narrow vision of obsessive accountants. Eager entry to the practice nets is exemplary; but prolonged occupation as the sun goes down and only a couple of aching servants and a schoolboy remain to bowl to him is, to say the least, unusual.

I do not suppose anyone has ever been as deeply committed, even addicted, to the business of batting as Geoff Boycott, and it will be a horrible wrench for him when the seven-day-a-week routine ends after twenty-odd years. Whatever he does with his remaining years, one wonder whether he can do it without first having an hour in the garden with someone to operate a bowling-machine, or a squad of bowlers – preferably well-paid.

What a vast galaxy of bowlers he has faced, and how proud are those who have captured his wicket, for it has been the hardest of all to obtain during the past two decades, even in charity and missionary games. Indeed, there may yet be many to add to the list, for while his eyes and reflexes last – there can be little question about his enthusiasm – he may bat on through the 1980s, getting ever nearer to Jack Hobb's pinnacle of 197 first-class centuries. Boycott met Herbert Sutcliffe, the gentleman player of Yorkshire and England, but he did not, so far as I know, meet Hobbs. Had he done so, he would have sensed immediately that here was a man of supreme modesty, kindness and gentleness, of whom it was said that you would never have thought, in conversing with him, that he had ever scored a run in his life. He made 61,237, actually, in first-class cricket.

Well, it takes all sorts. And if these remarks seem a tinge critical of Geoff Boycott, then they should be accompanied by the observation that I have seen him in 'fun' mood (though never at the crease). When apprehensive young Paul Allott was consigned to the boundary in the Old Trafford Test match of 1981, upon resumption after a bomb scare, 'Boycs' bade him farewell with the comforting promise that if Allott was blown up, he, Boycott, would see to it that his spectacles – if they were found – would be sent home to his Mum. I have also experienced his charm, a charm of the kind which, all the same, I couldn't help suspecting needed a little effort. Perhaps we all (apart from Ian Botham) take him too seriously, though it would be hard not to do so if you have just been run out through his instinct for self-preservation or thrown your wicket away while attempting to remedy the slack flow of runs. His supporters point to the glorious 146 he hit against Surrey in the 1965 Gillette Cup final, without always realising that this is the ultimate condemnation. The man *could* score fast when he chose. He *was* that good. Perhaps he was *not* just a self-made batsman with severe limitations. The limitations were self-imposed.

Cricket owes him something for keeping it on the front pages of the papers so often. The 'tragedy' is that while Yorkshire and England both also owe him much for the many times his bat has stood between them and defeat, the debt is rather obscured by the constant controversy surrounding the man. Looking back, does he regret that he did not work the gear-changes more skilfully? We are unlikely to find out.

Chris Clark, whose studies of the Test careers of Fred Trueman and

Sunil Gavaskar were of such value, has now bravely set himself the much more difficult task of appraising a complicated career, one seldom treated with a 'wart and all' approach. Boycott's batting may be the kind you're often happier to read about than sit through, but he has grafted together a very formidable set of career figures indeed, gathering runs as a miser drops coins into his coffers. Shylock and Fagin are outstanding figures in English literature. So let it be in English cricket for Geoffrey Boycott of Yorkshire.

DAVID FRITH
Guildford, December 1985

1 A good start

Geoffrey Boycott – the very name provokes passionate response. Indeed it often appears that those who are discussing him are engaged in a form of warfare. Boycott has never been far away from controversy and his admirers have followed him with the fanaticism of pop fans. In fact Boycott has attained the status of Superstar and this has kept him firmly in the public gaze.

With all deference to Boycott himself, the attention he has generated has led to the danger of the man becoming more important than the game itself; but this cannot in the end be good for cricket in general or for Boycott in particular.

Many people have allowed the situation to develop whereby there is no middle ground left in which to negotiate. Boycott himself, committees, selectors, a news-hungry media, an idolising public and those who have tried to get rid of him from the game have all helped to provoke the harshness of feeling, the lack of compromise. Such is the depth of the problem that it could be another twenty years before the last salvo in the battle has been fired and the dust finally settles over Geoffrey's career.

The heart of the Boycott imbroglio lies in his unwillingness to accept second best. In his work, Boycott's total dedication eventually brought him more runs than any previous batsman in Test history (until surpassed by India's S. M. Gavaskar in November 1983). He is a man who knows no half-measures and his followers reflect this attitude. For them, their hero can do no wrong. His detractors, however, are just as forceful in their contentions, and they too have the game of cricket at heart.

Boycott's career has been subject to controversy from his very first season in 1962. There have been good reasons for this and Boycott himself is not blameless, but it is time to view the man and his achievements in the context of the game of cricket as a whole and his contribution to it. For, as much as Boycott has been the sinner on various occasions, he has often been cast as the fall-guy, the easy target, a victim against whom it is all too easy to sin.

There is a sense in which many of his wounds are self-inflicted: one almost feels that Boycott possesses an in-built desire to arouse hostility. Yet, despite the traumas, he has come through it and triumphed where few other batsmen have triumphed. His fans are proud of his achievements and he has every reason to feel proud too.

He scored more Test runs than any previous batsman, a record that stood for two years. It matters not that this feat was later improved by another – the achievement of a world test record is a monument to his skill and dedication.

This argument does not impress his critics, who tend to see only the one side of his nature. Their attacks often appear to be vendettas and the net result has been in some quarters to make the man into cricket's *bête noire*.

In any discussion about Boycott the context within which his career is judged must be adjusted to take account of all the factors. If we accept that his personality is not his best asset, we must ensure that we consider his achievements.

At the end of the 1985 season Boycott had to his name 8,114 Test runs and 149 first-class centuries. However, in 1964, at the start of his career, he hit no less than eight centuries between May and November. Two years later, in the 1966 English season, he hit another six centuries. Eleven more followed between January and September 1968, and, as if that were not enough, in the same period during 1971, Boycott scored a staggering thirteen centuries.

Those were not simply the deeds of a very good batsman: they were performances of the highest calibre, achieved whilst playing against some of the best attacks that world cricket could offer. And, most important, they contained that most valuable ingredient – consistency. This was a master craftsman lovingly giving his best, a batsman who always strived to surpass his highest standards, and succeeded not once, but season after season, tour after tour. His career spanned two decades and his consistency followed him into the 1980s.

Of course he experienced bad times too, but he was remarkably durable and well equipped to overcome the rough times. His ability, temperament, technique, stamina, fitness, dedication and determination all helped him to rise above his problems and to return to his best. He was a batsman of class, much loved by the crowds, young and old alike, but given little credit within the cricket establishment.

I prefer to let his record speak for itself, and the best place to begin a study of it is at Bradford Park Avenue on 16 June 1962. That summer Saturday Geoffrey Boycott made his first-class Test debut for Yorkshire against the touring Pakistanis. As he awaited his turn at the crease, we can easily imagine him casting his mind back to 1950, when he was ten years old (he was born on October 21st 1940), winning a Len Hutton bat in a newspaper competition. What a portent!

The young Boycott was outstanding. At his village primary school in Fitzwilliam he once scored 45 runs out of a team total of 52. He followed this by demolishing the opposition with bowling figures of 6 for 10. This one match prompted an uncle, Mr Albert Speight, to suggest to the family that they should give Geoff an unusual eleventh birthday present.

They responded by paying 2s 6d each so that the boy could be coached at the Johnny Lawrence Indoor School in nearby Rothwell. Such was Geoff's progress that the family renewed the subscription annually.

Within a short space of time Boycott became captain of both his school team and the South Elmsall and District Schoolboy XI. For the latter team he managed to average 70 runs a game. By the age of thirteen, he was occasionally being chosen to play for Ackworth, a senior team in the Yorkshire Council. When he was fifteen he was captaining Yorkshire schoolboys, playing for Barnsley in the highest grade of Yorkshire club cricket, and had also been invited to the county's nets. Finally, when seventeen, he was selected to tour the Midlands with the Yorkshire Cricket Federation.

Rather less auspicious were Boycott's first appearances for the Yorkshire Second XI which were made in 1959 with games in each of the Minor Counties and Second IX competitions. His scores were 1*, 2, 5 and 15 respectively, but of much greater import was the innings of 88 he made for Barnsley against Leeds which had gained him selection for the Second IX. That batting display was seen by W. H. H. Sutcliffe, the former Yorkshire captain and son of Herbert Sutcliffe, who was then captaining Leeds. Subsequently, in 1960, when Boycott was incapacitated by a hamstring injury, Sutcliffe suggested that, when he was fit, Boycott might join Leeds. This he did and soon became their regular opener.

After missing that 1960 season, Boycott returned to the Yorkshire Second XI and made an immediate impact by scoring 156* against Cumberland. Again he was playing in both the Minor Counties and Second XI competitions although now he enjoyed more regular selection. From twenty innings Boycott averaged a shade more than 42 and accumulated well in excess of 600 runs. It was a very sound first season and when Cumberland was at the receiving end of his second century, 126*, at the start of 1962, Boycott was rewarded with his Yorkshire Second XI cap. Innings of 32 and 87* versus Northumberland, and 104* against Lancashire, followed in quick succession and it was this 'mini-Roses' hundred which clinched Boycott his place in the First XI against the Pakistanis at Bradford. With less than fifty Second Team innings to his credit, and with a season missed in between, Geoff found himself opening the batting for Yorkshire for the very first time. His first-class career was under way.

His time in the Second XI, including the full 1962 season, produced the following batting averages:

---

* Throughout this book I have followed the statistical custom of using an asterisk to denote a 'not out' innings.

	I	NO	Runs	HS	Avge	
1958	4	1	23	15	7.66	(Minor Counties & 2nd XI Comp)
1960	–	–	–	–	–	
1961	11	3	337	156	42.12	(Minor Counties)
	11	3	340	61	42.50	(2nd XI Competition)
1962	17	4	586	126	45.07	(Minor Counties)
	43	**11**	**1,266**	**156**	**39.56**	

Against the Pakistanis, however, he was not so successful. His initial first-class scores were:

1.	b. D'SOUZA 4
2. c. IMTIAZ AHMED	b. D'SOUZA 4

However, many another famous cricketer has started his first-class career with even less in the scorebook (Sir Leonard Hutton's duck for example!).

Boycott's first County Championship appearance came in the very next match, against Northampton. This began on 20 June, the day after the Pakistan fixture ended in a draw. This time Boycott batted at number four, from which position he made 6 and 21* in a game lost by 6 wickets with only five minutes playing time remaining. On that evidence he was retained in the side for the following county game at Chesterfield against Derbyshire where he opened the innings once again. His response was 47 and 30* in a drawn game. In Yorkshire's first innings he was caught behind the wicket by R. W. Taylor who, twenty years later, would be playing with Boycott when England faced the Indians at Calcutta.

After this match Boycott returned to the Second Team and he was offered only two more first-class appearances that season, in consecutive matches at the end of July and beginning of August. He scored 20 at Sheffield against Essex in an innings victory whilst, against Kent at Middlesbrough, he made 18 first time round and then received his first duck in first-class cricket, the bowler being Melville. At the end of the 1962 first-class season Boycott's record was as follows:

M	I	NO	Runs	HS	Avge
5	9	2	150	47	21.42

Despite its limitations, his performance, plus his consistent Second XI scoring, proved that he could fit into the First Team if required. The next season, following the departure of J. B. Bolus for Nottinghamshire, and an ankle injury to Ray Illingworth, Yorkshire found itself short of two quality players. Boycott helped to fill the gap in spectacular fashion. He scored 1,446 runs in the County Championship of 1963 with an average of 46.64. Thus he finished second only to M. J. K. Smith in the national averages, was the only Yorkshire player to score over 1,000 runs, and also achieved instant fame by hitting a century in each of the Roses fixtures. By any standards it was a highly satisfactory first full season.

In that first full season, Boycott moved up and down the batting order. Although he often opened, he seemed more at home in the middle of the order. Thus it was that his maiden first-class century, 145 versus Lancashire at Sheffield in early June, was made at number five. During that innings, which contained twenty-three boundaries, Boycott shared a mammoth partnership of 249 runs with W. B. Stott (143) which set up Yorkshire's innings victory.

By August, Boycott had once again reverted to opener. His second century (113) was scored whilst he was batting number one against Lancashire at Manchester. He had been re-established there the match before and subsequently that season he made scores of 62, 28, 113, 20*, 12, 0, 71, 13, 24, 8*, 90, 4, 1, 165*, 38, 64, 7 and 75. He had thus secured the place left vacant by Brian Bolus with a good season's work:

	M	I	NO	Runs	HS	Avge	100
County Championship	25	38	7	1,446	165*	46.64	3
All First-Class	28	43	7	1,682	165*	45.22	3

1963 was quite a year for Geoffrey Boycott and a fitting start for the career of one of the game's most remarkable batsmen.

2 Home and abroad

A singular event took place at the advent of the 1964 season which evoked amazement amongst Yorkshire supporters who always demand exceptional effort from their players. Boycott gave up his job as a wages clerk much sooner than was necessary in order to report for pre-season training with the County. Typically, the single-minded Boycott felt that he needed practice without the hindrance of full-time ordinary employment. He wasted no time during this period. In the mornings he attended the Yorkshire Schoolboys nets, in the afternoons the Colts and Senior coaching classes and in the evenings, away from Headingley, the nightly net sessions at the Leeds club. Four separate periods of practice per day and evidently he was still keen for more!

In the event, the full measure of Boycott's prosperity, the prize for painstaking practice and endeavour, was a glittering run of success that was not restricted to the 1964 English season. He began readily enough in May with 151 against Middlesex at Leeds but it was only a foretaste of what was to come as triumph followed triumph, stretching through into 1965 with a continual feast of runs. What was important was the variety of opposition. It showed Boycott's ability, as yet unproven, to adapt his play not only to different opposition in England but also against top-class players abroad, namely South Africa where he was touring in the winter 1964–5. The one lull in this progress occurred during June when a fractured finger kept him out of cricket.

For a player in only his second full season of first-class cricket the strides forward made by Boycott in 1964 were enormous. In early 1963 he had been an unheard-of middle order batsman. Less than a year later he had become an automatic first-choice opener for England; furthermore, there were few qualms from any part of the country that he was not the best person available for the position. But while that rapid elevation to Test status was in itself a meteoric rise in the career of any player, it formed no more than a quarter of the full story of 1964 and early 1965.

First, on the home front, Boycott scored 2,110 first-class runs (average 52.75) which was an increase of nearly 500 runs on his 1963 aggregate. As those runs came from just one extra first-class innings, 44 compared to 43, the significance was obvious. In the process, Boycott doubled his 1963 tally of three centuries to six in the latter year of 1964.

Second, there was Boycott's Test debut against Australia in June which he followed with a maiden Test hundred in the final match of the series.

The net result, and Boycott's third happy event of the year, was an assured place in the MCC touring party that was later announced to visit South Africa in the winter of 1964–5. He scored four hundreds on the trip, including a second in Tests, to which was added a fourth distinction which Boycott gained by being chosen as one of *Wisden*'s 'Five Cricketers of the Year' for 1964 when the 1965 edition was published. With the passing of the first three milestones that honour too would have appeared to have been a cut and dried affair; but without doubt, Boycott's initial impact on cricket was seen as dramatic not only by bowlers but by the writers who excitedly hailed a new batting star.

It was as early as May 1964 that the latter began reiterating their predictions from the previous season. Prior to the Test series against Australia, Boycott warmed to his forthcoming work with some very fine batting against Middlesex and Lancashire. His 151 versus the former at Leeds was followed by a third successive Roses hundred in consecutive matches against the latter when he made 131 at Old Trafford. Consequently, it was more or less taken for granted that he would be picked for England and the summons duly arrived when the team for the first Test was selected on 31 May. Boycott was in, but as if not content with mere selection and by way of celebration, he took 151* off Leicestershire during the match he was then currently playing in at Leicester. In the meantime, *The Times* correspondent had put his achievement into perspective: 'Boycott's rise to Test cricket has been remarkable,' he wrote. 'This time last year he was hidden away at No. 6 or 7, a little-known name. Now he was in everyone's team. He looks, at 23, to have a productive career ahead of him.'

While that future career was being predicted in terms of mass-production the first days of Boycott's and England's first Test was singularly unproductive although the few minutes play possible did not pass without incident. The weather at Trent Bridge allowed only eighty-five minutes play in all but during that brief period there was much to evoke comment. Even before play began there were problems, with John Edrich having to drop out of the team because of injury. Consequently, Boycott's first opening partner in Test cricket was the rather unlikely choice off-spin bowler Freddie Titmus.

Unlikely as the pair seemed, they performed very creditably. Titmus was no bottom number with a bat and although his was the solitary wicket to fall in the short playing period it did not occur until 38 runs had been added for the first wicket. That total, however, would have been considerably less had not Wally Grout, the Australian wicket-keeper, performed an act of sportsmanship of a type that has become difficult to envisage in the money-ridden Test cricket of the 1970s and 1980s.

By a quirk of coincidence, one of the most consistent criticisms made of Boycott over the years has been his calling and running between the wickets. The 'Titmus incident' occurred over just such a call for a quick single. Boycott had the 'bad caller' image attached to him from his very first Test. The action occurred when Boycott gently pushed a ball from Neil Hawke away and called for a sharp single. In the confusion that followed, Hawke, running through from his delivery-stride to retrieve the ball, inadvertently knocked Titmus to the ground. Graham Corling immediately swooped on the ball, hurled it to wicketkeeper Grout with Titmus helplessly stranded more than half-way down the wicket. Yet, Grout did no more than make a graceful pass over the top of the stumps with the ball and therefore allowed Titmus to reach the crease safely.

The original collision between Hawke and Titmus had been quite accidental but it made no difference to Grout – he obviously did not relish gaining wickets, even in a Test Match, in such a fashion. Norman O'Neill, standing at cover, made his famous comment of stunned amazement: 'Bloody hell, and I thought this was a Test Match', and to a degree, he had a point, but Grout's actions were nevertheless an object lesson for all cricketers. It is doubtful if such exemplary sportsmanship has ever been exceeded in Test cricket. Unfortunately for Boycott, his predilection for the risky single was not curbed by the incident which was to be only the first of many major occasions when his calling or running was to be faulted. Few would have a similar happy ending in the future.

Before the Titmus incident, Boycott had had a hard time in making his first appearance for England. His chief tormentor was Hawke, who bowled particularly well in the wet conditions and made Boycott play and miss three times before he eventually got off the mark with a thick edge past third slip for 4. Boycott was also dropped at third slip by Booth, again off Hawke, but Boycott remained commendably phlegmatic waiting only for the next ball and concentrating on that rather than worrying about the previous delivery. Therefore, when play was called off for the day Boycott remained at the crease with 23 to his name and the England total standing at 52 for 1.

The second day saw an improvement in the weather. Ninety-five minutes was the total of lost time and in the morning session Boycott scored all of the first 15 runs added to the overnight total. They came mainly from McKenzie full-tosses which, but for the rain-sodden turf slowing down the well-struck ball, would have yielded considerably more. In a shade more than one hour's batting Boycott added 25 to his own score. Then, at 48, and within touching distance of a half-century on his debut, Corling produced a perfect outswinger that found the edge of the bat and Simpson, diving far away to his right at first slip, took a brilliant one-handed catch. In all, Boycott had batted for two-and-a-half hours in the most taxing conditions against some hostile and very accurate bowling. In doing so, he had shown a resolution and tenacity which drew much praise from the critics:

G. BOYCOTT   c. SIMPSON   b. CORLING   48

When the third day of his debut Test was also lost to rain, the game became doomed to be drawn. On the fourth day, after England declared at 216 for 8, Australia were bowled out relatively cheaply for 168 but there was insufficient time left, even with another declaration, to bowl the Aussies out a second time. Unfortunately, during what time there was for play on the fourth day Boycott fractured a finger while fielding, which put paid to any further participation by him in the match.

The injury kept him out of the second Test at Lord's, which was also drawn, so that the satisfaction of a pleasing debut was tempered by the irritation of enforced inactivity just at the time when Boycott was in prime form. Conversely his return to the Test team when he was again fully fit was assured, and when it did occur, for the third Test, it would be at his home ground of Headingley. This would help in some way to compensate for missing the Lord's Test. Alas, the result would not.

Headingley produced the one definite result of the series – which earned the title of 'Burge's Match'. This was for the way Peter Burge turned seeming defeat into stunning victory with a marvellously inventive innings of 160 when he had no more than three partners left in the Australian first innings. Long before Burge took charge of the crease, England had batted first to reach a rather disappointing total of 268 all out by close of play, of which Boycott's contribution had been an impressive 38.

Boycott opened with John Edrich, who in time would become one of his most successful partners in Test cricket. On this occasion neither scored any runs in the first 3 overs and then, in stark contrast, Boycott cut loose with a flurry of strokes to take three boundaries in quick succession off Graham McKenzie. The score advanced to 17 before Edrich fell to a mistimed hook which saw the ball loop gently off his glove straight into the hands of backward short leg. Boycott, however, continued imperturbably. He was particularly strong on the off-side, around the cover area, and in reaching 38 without being unduly worried set the scene for a large Boycott score. The hard work had been accomplished, the worst of the new-ball shine had been taken off, and Boycott looked to be in command when he was tempted forward to an outswinger from Corling: the same edge, the same expert slip Simpson and the same Corling had combined to produce a replica of Trent Bridge with the slight difference this time that Boycott made 10 runs less.

To rub salt into the wound Simpson and Corling united again in the second innings to remove Boycott for 4 and thus performed a rare type of 'hat-trick', the third successive dismissal of Boycott in two Tests. That occurred on the third day, following Burge's great innings, and Simpson's third Boycott catch was another beautiful effort. He had to dive a long way to his left towards wicketkeeper Grout and once again took the ball one-handed in response to Corling's outswing.

By close of play, 3 more wickets fell as the score rose to 157, an amount that gave England a meagre lead of only 36 runs with just 6 wickets left. On the fourth day an indecisive all-out total of 229 presented Australia with a target of only 109 runs for victory. Duly accomplished, with 7 wickets in hand, this meant that the Ashes were as good as on their way back to the Antipodes.

Bobby Simpson was largely responsible for the destiny of the Ashes. The fourth Test, played at Old Trafford, became meaningless when Australia amassed 611 in a first innings that lasted well into the third day. Simpson scored a triple century yet, incredibly, his 311 was his maiden Test hundred. The Aussie tactics could not be faulted; they did lead in the series but the words of one of the English participants, Peter Parfitt, summed up the situation precisely: 'It was the most boring Test Match I ever played in.' Fewer than 20 wickets fell in the whole game and the sad irony for Boycott was that he missed the opportunity of such a perfect batting strip to accumulate the kind of score in the manner which later became his trademark.

England actually passed Australia's total, reaching 656 for 8 declared, and Boycott actually scored his first half-century in Test cricket. In fact, he had scored 58 when, almost sensationally, Graham McKenzie bowled him out with an outstanding delivery. He produced the type of delivery no batsman could rightfully expect on that type of wicket. The ball pitched on the middle stump, moved away wickedly and took the off stump. Boycott was as bemused as he had been at Headingley when Corling trapped him when similarly well-entrenched at the crease.

That score of 58 meant that, although Boycott had performed with credit in his three Tests, he had seemingly failed to capitalise on three sound starts from four innings, particularly at Manchester. No doubt he felt the disappointment strongly himself. Thus it was that at the Oval in the final Test the situation was corrected in typically forthright style. Once more rain badly interfered with play, taking away all of the last day at a point when England might have won but, the result excepted, the game turned into a Yorkshire triumph. Prior to Boycott's second innings century, his county colleague Fred Trueman had, on the third day, hoisted his personal tally of Test wickets to the previously thought impossible total of 300 when he had Neil Hawke caught by Cowdrey in the slips.

Hawke always maintained that he would be remembered for nothing else in Test cricket but for the fact that he was Trueman's 300th victim in

Tests, but he did himself less than justice for his contribution to the Oval Test. With a then career-best haul of 6 for 47, Hawke was the prime reason for England's dismal first innings total of 182 all out on the first day. Boycott had begun the game with a flourish, hitting McKenzie's first ball to the boundary and he went on to 30 before being bowled by Hawke, and from that point the initiative was with, and remained with, Australia until the fourth day.

By the end of the second day Australia had progressed to 245 for 5 and subsequently, despite Trueman's achievement the total was hoisted to 379 all out, which gave the Aussies an impressive lead of 197 runs. It was at this juncture that Boycott came into his own to fulfil the promise of his earlier innings in the series. He began with an opening partnership which produced 80 runs. More significantly, he still occupied the crease when stumps were drawn with England on 132 for 2. The scene was thus set for his maiden Test hundred and on the fourth day Boycott did not disappoint his growing army of fans. Not until the score reached 255 was Boycott dismissed, fourth out, after batting five hours and producing an innings that was full of fine strokes, particularly drives and square-cuts. That innings:–

G. BOYCOTT   c. REDPATH   b. SIMPSON   113

was the crowning glory of his season.

With play washed out on the last day (when England held a lead of 184 runs with 6 wickets in hand) a rather disappointing series dripped rather than dropped into the record books. Nevertheless, Boycott could look back with considerable satisfaction. Nearly 300 runs in his first series, at an average of almost 50 per innings, was certainly a sound foundation on which to build. But he still had much to prove before he could show that the promise and hopes were not misplaced. In the event, there was little to worry about on that score; the tour of South Africa would see to that.

Averages for 1964 Series v Australia

Tests	I	NO	Runs	HS	Avge
4	6	0	291	113	48.50

Bowling: 1–0–3–0		**Centuries:** 1	
Fielding: 0		**Half-Centuries:** 1	

Before Boycott could turn his thoughts fully towards South Africa there was still the domestic season for him to complete. At the beginning, through till June, he had hit three centuries for Yorkshire and a similar spell ensued from August onwards, commencing shortly before the last Test. To the chagrin of the Tourists, the Test hundred was his second such effort in consecutive matches against them, for Boycott had profited to the tune of 122 runs from the Australian attack at Bradford. Thence to The Oval and next, to round off the season in rousing style, he slammed Gloucestershire's bowlers for a career-best of 177 at Bristol. It augured well for South Africa; so well indeed that the newly made personal top score lasted until no later than the fifth game of the tour.

The tour began in mid-October. With the Tests not due to commence until the beginning of December there was a good settling-in period available to the MCC squad containing six first-class matches before the first Test, giving ample time to adjust to the new conditions. Boycott played in all those matches. His run of scores from those games (17, 4, 38, 53, 17, 14, 8*, 193*, 106 and 0) show that it was not until the fifth fixture that he struck anything like his best form. On paper at least, therefore, it would appear that the long run-in to the series proper was beneficial to Boycott in allowing him time to adapt to a cricketing environment he was encountering for the first time.

Of the six games, the two which provided centuries were obviously the most important to Boycott. From another point of view, as if to emphasise the total uncertainty of cricket, the second match of the tour is also worthy of note for it very nearly produced a shock defeat for MCC by only half a team! In the opening fixture Rhodesia had been comfortably defeated by 5 wickets and a young Colts XI, in theory, should not have presented any great problems in the next match. However, a foretaste of events to come was hammered home to the MCC team in the Colts' first innings when two future Test players, Botten and Macaulay, hit a century stand for the last wicket at a rate of 2 runs a minute.

The Colts closed at 393 all out and summarily gained a first innings lead of 126 runs by dismissing MCC for 267. Boycott's contribution to this was 38 in the first innings and 13 in the second. The problems were mounting for the tourists but disaster struck the Colts after they had reached 61 without loss by the end of the second day. Illness struck down two players so that only nine men could bat for the team and after their dismissal set MCC a victory target of 293 runs. Further injuries during the course of the match depleted the Colts to a skeleton outfit. At one stage they had no fewer than six substitutes on the field, including two Englishmen, and had only two bowlers available, Crookes and MacKay-Coghill. Yet, they still had MCC tottering on the brink of defeat. Crookes in particular, with his off-spin, was very steady. He claimed 5 for 102 from 38 overs and although some batsmen got themselves out attempting to force the pace it was a day of almost unparalleled humiliation for MCC who were extremely relieved to reach the close with 2 wickets remaining, their score being 241 for 8.

Against Western Province the ball ran much more kindly. Boycott's 193 not out was made off an attack including Test bowlers Peter Pollock, Barlow and Dumbrill. The innings included a huge fourth wicket partnership of 278 runs with his skipper, Mike Smith (153), which lasted four hours and that was exactly half of the time Boycott spent at the crease. He followed up with 106 against Western Province although a 0 in the second innings redressed the balance for the bowlers. However, with those two centuries, Boycott had made as good a start as could be expected to his first tour. He had 450 runs from six games and ten innings and, apart from the last innings 0, he had prepared himself very satisfactorily for the first Test. Furthermore, when that game got under way those preparatory strikes paid handsome dividends.

England went to Durban without a victory in any of their previous twelve Test matches. The pundits were well and truly surprised, therefore, when South Africa were beaten by an innings and 104 runs. The main criticism before the tour began, and one borne out in retrospect, was that the pace attack of Cartwright, Price, Thomson and Brown would be largely ineffective. How a bowler of Trueman's calibre could be passed over in favour of these players still appears inexplicable. Fortunately, at Durban, the spinners held the upper hand and after some excellent batting Titmus and Allen gained England's unexpected prize.

Boycott and Barber set England on their route to victory with what was the first of only two century partnerships they achieved in the twenty-six times they opened together for England. They stroked 120 runs at Durban before Goddard bowled Barber for 74 and Boycott fell a little later for one run less, trapped leg-before by Partridge. Once again it was a highly satisfying 'first' for Boycott, and he was the ideal foil to Barber's wristy, innovative flair which was so exciting to watch. When in full flow Barber could tear any attack apart. Perhaps his style did not lend itself to the building of regular large opening stands; nevertheless, he was still one of Boycott's most successful opening partners.

At Durban, the flying start the pair had given England set the scene for Barrington (148*) and Parks (108*) to complete England's stranglehold on the game. Their unbroken stand of 206 runs for the sixth wicket was a record in England–South Africa Tests, taking England to 485 for 5 declared on the second day. When the Springboks lost Goddard, Barlow and Graham Pollock for 20 runs by close of play the issue was virtually settled. South Africa, 155 all out, were forced to follow-on 330 runs behind England, and only Colin Bland, that superb fielder, with 68, remained defiant as South Africa again capitulated. Shortly after lunch on the fourth day England had won without having to bat a second time. After the initial onslaught by Boycott, Barber, Barrington and Parks, the spinners, Titmus and Allen, with 13 wickets between them guided England to a well-earned victory, and with it went the ultimate prize of the rubber in the series. Both events were extremely, though very pleasantly, surprising.

Historically, with all the remaining four Tests being drawn, the series appears dull, yet there was plenty of tension and excitement in the games, especially for Boycott. In the second and third tests he scored only 4, 15 and 1* but in the latter game Boycott the bowler stepped forward. In fact, throughout his career, Boycott was always a more than useful seam-up bowler and in South Africa, possibly because of the limited resources at his disposal, Mike Smith employed him more regularly than he was used at any other time in his career, either for England or Yorkshire. In the third Test it is not difficult to see why. In South Africa's second innings Boycott claimed from 20 overs 3 for 47 and two at least of his victims are worthy of special mention:

R. G. POLLOCK		b. BOYCOTT	73
K. C. BLAND		b. BOYCOTT	64
S. F. BURKE	c. BARBER	b. BOYCOTT	20

Pollock and Bland were Boycott's first Test wickets. And clean bowled into the bargain!!

While his bowling could be looked upon as something of a bonus it was in the fourth Test at Johannesburg that Boycott's forte as a batsman shone through, and in the process he saved a Test Match for England. It was, in his eight-Test career so far, by far his best performance. In playing terms in general, there was little to choose between the sides on the evidence of the first innings. Rain had taken away three-and-a-quarter hours from the first two days by which time South Africa had declared at 390 for 6 and England replied with 384 all out, due mainly to 122 not out from Peter Parfitt. Boycott made just 5 at the first attempt but at the second time of asking nothing and nobody could move him.

By declaring at 307 for 3 Goddard tempted Smith and his team to score 314 runs in four hours to win. Without the services of Barber, who had chipped a bone in his finger whilst fielding, Smith was never going to take up the challenge and, as wickets fell around him, only Boycott remained between South Africa and victory. For all of the four hours Boycott occupied the crease; inanimate, immovable. At the close, the scoreboard showed England to be 153 for 6 and without Boycott's stonewalling 76 not out, the series would undoubtedly have been level.

From Johannesburg the series moved to its conclusion at Port Elizabeth. In between the Tests Boycott emphasised his good form by hitting 114 off a South African Invitation XI at Cape Town and then went 3 runs better in the first innings of the final Test. At Port Elizabeth, Boycott's 117 ensured that England batted until tea on the fourth day in reply to South Africa's 502 all out. With just four sessions of play remaining there was insufficient time for South Africa to force the issue and bowl England out again. They made the effort, declaring at lunch on the last day but, whichever way the game may have gone, rain caused play to be abandoned, and England were left victors in the series.

The tour was a personal triumph for Boycott. No less an authority than *Wisden* commented: 'Of the young, comparatively untried players, none was able to force his way irresistibly to the fore as Boycott of

Yorkshire had done in a matter of two years. From fifteen matches on the tour Boycott aggregated 1,135 runs and only Barrington of the other batsmen also passed the one-thousand mark.'

No player can remain in top form all the time, however, and now Boycott's fortunes were about to change.

Averages for 1964–65 Series v South Africa

Tests	I	NO	Runs	HS	Avge
5	8	2	298	117	49.66

Bowling: 61–16–157–5   **Centuries:** 1
Fielding: 2   **Half-Centuries:** 2

Cumulative Test Career Averages

Tests	I	NO	Runs	HS	Avge
9	14	2	589	117	49.08

Bowling: 62–16–160–5   **Centuries:** 2
Fielding: 2   **Half-Centuries:** 3

3 Fluctuating fortunes

In Boycott's first three full seasons of first-class cricket, incuding the South African tour, he had scored 5,023 runs and hit thirteen centuries. It was impressive by any measure and showed above-average steadiness and resolve. But in 1965 he fell short of his own standards. It was characteristic of the man that he always chided himself when things did not go well with his cricket. Many county players would probably have been quite happy, however, to have Boycott's averages for the season.

In fact, he topped the County Championship averages for Yorkshire with 942 runs at 34.88. Injuries and Test calls had restricted his championship appearances to seventeen matches – just over half the full programme. If all first-class games are considered then Boycott still passed the thousand mark without difficulty to achieve 1,447 runs at 35.29. However, it was the mark of an indifferent season for him that this was achieved without a single century.

To add to Boycott's dissatisfaction, he was dropped for the first time by England during the South African visit. Despite this, he fought back with characteristic determination and came good at the end of the season. There were two separate Test series that year against New Zealand and South Africa. On the Test front the situation was little improved from the County Championship. Only against the Kiwis did Boycott achieve a modicum of success, which was somewhat ironic, for throughout his career New Zealand has rarely presented easy runs for him; in fact his record against the New Zealanders was often dismal. Yet on the first occasion he encountered them he averaged 52.33 from four innings. In later series even double figures would have been a blessing which proves how even the best can struggle against what was regarded as weak opposition.

In the first Test of the summer, at Edgbaston, the freezing weather was the main talking point, apart from England's 9-wicket victory. Few Tests can have been played in colder weather; and it was one of the rare occasions when *hot* drinks had to be served *twice* on the field during a Test in England. Another topic of discussion was Barrington's monumental innings of 137 spread over seven-and-a-half hours. As a result Barrington was summarily dropped for the next Test, and it was a salutory lesson which Boycott also would have done well to heed. He himself incurred a similar penalty for the same offence only two years later.

At Edgbaston, Boycott's share was 23 and 44*, the former being part of England's all out total of 435 which included Barrington's snail-paced century. After New Zealand followed on 319 runs behind, the Arctic weather was the sole factor that might have prevented England from winning.

New Zealand batted much better in their second innings but their very creditable 413 not out was less than one hundred ahead of England's total. The victory was duly accomplished on the last morning. Barber (51) attempted to go out in a blaze of glory by hitting a six, but was caught in the deep by the substitute Vivian. This meant that the lead was reduced to only 9 wickets. However, Boycott promptly hit the next ball straight to the boundary.

It was at Headquarters that Boycott played his best Test of the summer. His innings of 76 in England's second innings, together with Dexter's 80*, was instrumental in gaining a 7-wicket victory for his team with just fifteen minutes playing time remaining. The match was a combination of another fine New Zealand recovery and bad weather, with the latter almost preventing a home victory. On the first day the Kiwis were dismissed for 175 but hit back before the close to dismiss both Boycott (14) and Barber (13). Recovering from that setback England reached 307 all out. Defeat was not reasonably possible but New Zealand's second innings 347, in harness with the loss of two hours on the fourth day and three on the fifth, made England's target of 215 to win extremely difficult.

Boycott and Dexter were England's answer to the problem. The pair had been together when Boycott had shared his very first century partnership in Test cricket (111 for the second wicket versus Australia at Old Trafford in 1964) but that had been in a match doomed to eternal boredom. At Lord's the chase was on and they hit 126 runs in just two-and-a-quarter hours before Boycott was trapped leg-before by Motz. The thrilling run-a-minute spree, where Boycott kept pace with the dashing Dexter, saw England home and, in the context of the season as a whole, it concluded a fair series for Boycott in good style. His innings ended lbw to Motz.

Of statistical value to Boycott was his 50-plus average from four innings; but he had no opportunity to improve on that in the third and final Test against the New Zealanders for he was injured a week before the game was due to start.

Strangely it was against England's second visitors of the summer that the injury occurred, namely South Africa. Playing against the Springboks for Yorkshire at Sheffield in a match plagued by run-outs (there were seven in all, five from Yorkshire) Boycott dived full-length, in vain, to save himself from precisely that fate only to strain his shoulder rather badly. In fact, in both innings against the South Africans Boycott suffered the same dismissal – run out!

Averages for 1965 Series v New Zealand

Tests	I	NO	Runs	HS	Avge
2	4	1	157	76	52.33

Bowling: **Centuries:** 0
Fielding: 0   **Half-Centuries:** 1

Cumulative Test Career Averages

Tests	I	NO	Runs	HS	Avge
11	18	3	746	117	49.73

Bowling: 62–16–160–5   **Centuries:** 2
Fielding: 2   **Half-Centuries:** 4

Boycott regained his Test place for the series against South Africa at the expense of Peter Parfitt who had played twice against New Zealand. Barber opened the innings with Boycott, and with Edrich at number three, Boycott edged out the Middlesex batsman to open in what was the one hundredth Test encounter between England and South Africa. In every sense the game was a thriller, packed with excitement from the start to finish. Less thrilling was Boycott's 31 and 28 in each innings respectively, but nobody batted outstandingly in the match; there were no centuries and only six men passed 50.

England took a first innings lead of 58 runs (338 to 280), but in the second innings their target amounted to no more than 191 runs, in five minutes under four hours. However, a slow over rate plus a bad injury to Edrich, hit on the head by a ball from Peter Pollock, hindered them. The South Africans performed well, claiming wickets at regular intervals and England steadily slipped behind the clock. At the close, with their score at 145 for 7, England were struggling to save a game which ended as an honours-even draw.

It was the second Test at Trent Bridge which brought about Boycott's downfall and the loss of his England place. The result scarcely helped matters: a victory to South Africa by 94 runs due largely to the combined brilliance of the Pollock brothers, but that was not the sole reason. It was more a case of Boycott's batting in the second innings; his effort, or apparent lack of it, drew loud criticism from many quarters. In South Africa, less than a year earlier, he had batted in exactly the same way to save a Test for England. Then, the praise had been tumultuous. Now the result was expulsion. However, the circumstances at Lord's, particularly towards the end of the game, do suggest that Boycott's lengthy occupation of the crease proved detrimental to England's chances of victory.

By the time Boycott went to the crease for a second time (after a first innings 'duck') England required 319 runs to win with two full days, plus thirty-five minutes from the third day, remaining. Those final thirty-five minutes of the third day proved critical. First Barber and then the nightwatchman, Titmus, fell before close. The die was cast, especially as Snow was sent in with a brief similar to Titmus'. Boycott was now the focal point but Mike Smith, the captain, was heavily criticised for using two nightwatchmen. The use of an established batsman at the fall of Titmus' wicket might have prevented a second wicket falling. Also, Snow batting at number four relegated Parks, a fine attacking batsman, to number nine in the order. Thus, the situation facing Boycott when he went out to bat with Snow on the fourth morning was a difficult one. Worse was to follow. Snow was dismissed without addition to the score and Barrington soon suffered the same fate. England's score was 13 for 4 wickets.

In effect the game was already lost, and this may explain the tactics which Boycott adopted. He took two hours and twenty minutes to score a mere 16 runs. For this he was roundly condemned on all sides. Athol McKinnon then put him and everyone out of their misery by penetrating Boycott's defence and hitting the stumps.

What had been needed to raise spirits was a bold defiance. Peter Parfitt showed what was possible by hitting the bowling to all parts of the ground. He eventually made 86, and Parks made 44*. They showed what was possible. Parks took 10 from 1 over from Dumbrill, and the pair made 27 runs between them off the first 3 overs of the new ball. The contrast between their performances and that of Boycott was dramatic. He could hardly complain at then being dropped by the England selectors.

In the event, his exclusion from the third Test should not have caused Boycott too much worry. Between the second and third Tests, on Sunday 15 August, the touring party for Australia was announced. Boycott's name was included, although *The Times* correspondent saw fit to add: 'There will, I think, be a word in Boycott's ear before he takes off for Australia to the effect that his approach at Lord's and Trent Bridge was not what England were looking for.'

Averages for 1965 Series v South Africa

Tests	I	NO	Runs	HS	Avge
2	4	0	75	31	18.75

Bowling: 26–10–60–0   **Centuries: 0**
Fielding: 0   **Half-Centuries: 0**

Cumulative Test Career Averages

Tests	I	NO	Runs	HS	Avge
13	22	3	821	117	43.21

Bowling: 88–26–220–5   **Centuries: 2**
Fielding: 2   **Half-Centuries: 4**

Ironically enough, the perfect answer to Boycott's critics came from him himself at Lord's in September, during the Gillette Cup Final. He gave a thrilling display – perhaps one of the greatest ever innings in this tournament (now called the NatWest Trophy). The tie was against Surrey. Heavy rain on the Friday meant that the match commenced ninety minutes late on the Saturday morning. Yorkshire were invited to bat and Ken Taylor was dismissed at 22. Then Boycott and Close took control. At the end of the allotted 60 overs, Yorkshire had scored 317 for 4. Three records had been created on the way. First, 317 was the highest total made in the final at that date; second, Boycott's stand with Close of 192 for the second wicket was also a record in the final; and third, Boycott's score of 146 was the highest individual score in a final, and remains so at the time of writing (1985).

During that innings, showing an attacking style which most spectators would have liked to have seen more frequently, Boycott struck three sixes and fifteen fours. That one innings, one of Boycott's best ever, proved conclusively that he did not need to be a dour, obstinate batsman. He could be both aggressive and entertaining and, what is more, he had a range of strokes which meant that he could tailor his innings to suit each occasion. His display at Lord's in 1965 was a virtuoso performance. What a pity it has not more often been repeated.

Scorecard of Gillette Cup Final Played at Lord's September 1965

Yorkshire

G. Boycott	c. Storey	b. Barrington	146
K. Taylor	c. Barrington	b. Sydenham	9
D. B. Close*	c. Edrich	b. Gibson	79
F. S. Trueman		b. Arnold	24
J. H. Hampshire		Not Out	38
D. Wilson		Not Out	11
		Extras B 3 LB 4 NB 3	10
		TOTAL (for 4 wickets) off 60 overs	317

D. E. V. Padgett, P. J. Sharpe, R. Illingworth, R. A. Hutton and J. G. Brinks† did not bat.

Fall of Wickets

1	2	3	4
22	214	248	292

Bowling	O	M	R	W
Arnold	13	3	51	1
Sydenham	13	1	67	1
Gibson	13	1	66	1
Storey	13	2	33	0
Tindall	3	0	36	0
Barrington	5	0	54	1

Surrey

M. J. Stewart*	ST. Binks	b. Wilson	33
J. H. Edrich	c. Illingworth	b. Trueman	15
W. A. Smith	LBW	b. Trueman	0
K. F. Barrington	c. Binks	b. Trueman	0
R. A. E. Tindall	c. Wilson	b. Close	57
S. J. Storey	LBW	b. Illingworth	1
M. J. Edwards		b. Illingworth	0
D. Gibson	LBW	b. Illingworth	0
A. Long†		b. Illingworth	17
G. Arnold		Not Out	3
D. A. D. Sydenham		b. Illingworth	8
		Extras B 4 LB 4	8
		TOTAL off 40.4 overs	142

Fall of Wickets

1	2	3	4	5	6	7	8	9	10
27	27	27	75	76	76	76	130	132	142

Bowling	**O**	**M**	**R**	**W**
Trueman	9	0	31	3
Hutton	8	3	17	0
Wilson	9	0	45	1
Illingworth	11.4	1	29	5
Close	3	0	12	1

*Captain †Wicket-Keeper

Yorkshire won by 175 runs
Man of the Match: G. Boycott
Adjudicator: D. J. Insole,
　　　　　Chairman of the England Selection Committee

Six weeks later Boycott was in Australia. It was his first visit and his preparations had been badly hampered by illness and injury. Of the six first-class matches which led up to the first Test, Boycott could play in only two. However, by the time of his first innings he had conquered a stomach complaint, sciatica, and back trouble too. In the third game of the tour, against South Australia, his game was little impaired. With Edrich as his partner 116 runs were scored for the first wicket. After Edrich left, Boycott continued strongly, to make 94. He did not bat in the second innings, nor did he play again until Queensland provided the opposition immediately prior to the first Test. In a drawn game he made 30 and 0.

Boycott was originally put down to bat at number six in an attempt to cover his lack of match practice and fitness. However Eric Russell split his right hand whilst fielding and Boycott was reinstated as an opener: a position he held for the rest of the tour.

At Brisbane, rain limited play to less than three hours on the first day. Australia then batted for more than nine hours, well into the fourth day, to make 443 for 6 declared and thus ruled out any meaningful outcome.

In England's first innings Boycott made 45. Together with half-centuries from Barrington, Parks and Titmus the time consumed meant that the follow-on could not be enforced until under four hours remained on the last day. The draw was virtually secure and, if there were any lingering doubts concerning England's position, Boycott put paid to them. He stayed at the crease for the full time of England's second innings and his 63* was well supported by Barber (34) and Edrich (37) to take England to 186 for 3 by close of play. Boycott, if not actually saving England, had gone a long way towards ensuring the draw.

As Australia had batted into the fourth day at Brisbane, so England followed suit at Melbourne but only after dismissing Australia for 358 in their first innings. England's answer was 558 but they took too long about it. At the outset Boycott (51) and Barber (48) gave their side a flying start with 98 runs in only 16 overs. Although Boycott was badly missed at slip in McKenzie's first over he took but seventy-six minutes to compile another half-century. Batting with the extrovert Barber that was a good rate of scoring but the rest of the team failed to carry on in the same style and batted too slowly. Edrich, for instance, spent five hours compiling a century. Not the sort of batting to produce victory.

With a first innings lead of 200 runs England were in a position to win the Test, but the missing of a simple off-side stumping chance by Parks put paid to such hopes. The batsman was Burge, the unfortunate bowler Barber; and from his then score of 34, Burge moved on to 120 before falling victim to Boycott. His innings ensured safety for Australia. Ironically, when Boycott claimed a second wicket to produce his best bowling figures against Australia, the batsman, Vievers, was stumped by Parks. If only it had been Burge!

Boycott's bowling figures, 9–0–32–2, are interesting not just for the fact that he took 2 wickets but because those wickets were the last he took in Test cricket – and he still had sixteen years of his Test career left! M. J. K. Smith was the only captain who seems to have recognised Boycott's potential as a stop-gap seam-up bowler, and he bowled Boycott (in South Africa, Australia and at home) far more than has any other captain.

The Melbourne Test was bound for a drawn conclusion long before the close of play. When Australia were finally all out there was but ten minutes batting time left for England which Boycott used to add 5 rather meaningless runs to this aggregate while Barber did not even bother to open his account. How different that would be in Sydney, venue of the third Test.

In retrospect, the winning of the toss by Smith at Sydney was generally reckoned to be the decisive factor in deciding the issue, but no less decisive was the brilliant batting of Barber and Boycott. Their opening stand was breathtaking, particularly Barber's share, and he played the greatest innings of his career for England. The pair complemented each other perfectly and, as the pitch progressively favoured spin, their opening gambit gave England an upper hand which was held throughout the match. Before being parted, the scoreboard had raced to 234, at which point Boycott gave a return catch to the leg-spinner, Philpott. From the outset the batting was almost storybook material, a thrill a minute. The only blemish came when Boycott was dropped at backward short-leg off the luckless McKenzie once again, with only 12 to his name. From that point onwards Barber and his less invigorating partner reigned supreme.

In the two hours to lunch, 93 runs were scored off 36 overs, followed afterwards by 141 in two hours. Boycott then departed, having scored 84 in four hours. The fifteenth run scored by Boycott during his innings represented his one thousandth Test run, those runs having been scored in sixteen Tests at an average of more than 40 per innings.

Another batsman scoring heavily for England was John Edrich who took Boycott's place at the wicket. He went on to make his second successive Test hundred, 103, while Barber eventually fell to Neil Hawke, bowled for 185, his innings lasting for four minutes less than five hours; it included nineteen boundaries and was rightly acclaimed as one of the greatest displays of controlled, forceful batting seen in Australia for many, many years.

Having dismissed Barber, Hawke ran through England's middle order. He finished with figures of 33.7–6–105–7, the best return of his Test career. However, his marathon effort came too late to save his team. Barber and Boycott, in setting up England's 488 all out, had put the game out of their reach. Strangely, although the pitch was more inclined to spin as the game progressed, it was not one of the slower bowlers but the paceman David Brown who wrecked Australia's hopes. His 5 for 63 reduced Australia to 221 all out in their first innings, while Titmus and Allen each took 4 wickets in the second innings. Australia, 174 all out, were still 93 runs short of England's total. Momentarily, therefore, England's innings victory gave them fleeting thoughts of returning home with the Ashes.

Because of inept tour planning, which provided no real opportunity for practice between the third and fourth Tests, Australia were quickly able to dash such hopes. The tables were turned when the Aussies replied with an equally impressive innings triumph. In between the two Tests, the MCC played against a Northern New South Wales County

Districts XI, Tasmania and a Combined XI. It was not the correct preparation for a Test Match although Boycott took advantage of the match against the Combined XI, at Hobart, to register his one first-class century, 156, of the tour.

Following the up-country games, the Test issue was put beyond doubt quite early at Adelaide when England were bowled out for 241 and Simpson (225) and Lawry (119) passed the score without being parted. England's troubles began with the loss of Barber, Edrich and Boycott (22) for only 33 runs. McKenzie's 6 for 48 meant that a large total was never feasible. Conversely, with the aid of Australia's highest first-wicket in Test cricket (their 244 remains a record in 1985) Simpson and Lawry opened up the possibility of an easy innings win. Their 516 all out was far too many for England. Hawke was the destroyer the second time around, with 5 for 54, but England kept a depressing sense of proportion by beginning in exactly the same manner as their first innings. Three wickets went down for 32 runs, including Boycott's for a modest 12. What followed must have left Boycott wondering about all the criticism he had had to endure when he was dropped against South Africa for showing a lack of initiative.

Barrington and Cowdrey were the culprits. The former hit only four boundaries during a five-and-a-half hour century while Cowdrey reached the fence just twice in two-and-a-half hours which produced a paltry 35 runs. Defensive tactics were of little use with two full days remaining as England began their second innings. Yet, Boycott, for employing the self-same tactics against South Africa the previous summer, had been publicly castigated and dismissed from the team. Now, Barrington and Cowdrey were allowed to get away with similar performances. As a result, it should not perhaps be too surprising that in later years Boycott appeared to have a chip on his shoulder.

At the end of the day, the tactics used at Adelaide were of no consequence. Simpson and Lawry, together with McKenzie and Hawke, were batting and bowling combinations which England could not beat. Nor could they beat the Australians in the final Test at Melbourne. From the humiliation of a defeat by an innings and 9 runs, England were forced to endure a boring draw to conclude the series and the extent of the boredom can be judged from the fact that less than 20 wickets fell. Lawry and Cowper strangled the game in pitiful fashion after England had made 485 for 9 declared. Lawry took more than six hours over 108 runs; Cowper, not to be outdone, batted for twelve hours and seven minutes to record a rare Test triple century, but his 307 contained only twenty boundaries. However, with the Ashes at stake, Australia's aim was not to lose. Therefore, if not excused, the Aussie methods could not really be faulted. Australia kept the Ashes.

Away from the actual result, the series ended in disaster for Boycott. Once again he had to contend with a barrage of criticism but on this occasion the facts tended to support the critics. As so often in his career, the issue centred around the plausible assumption that Boycott was prone to 'hogging' the bowling and was Danger personified when it came to running between the wickets. Sadly, to take Melbourne as an example, there was more than a grain of truth in the accusation. In the England first innings Boycott took sixty of the first eighty deliveries; or, nearly 8 of the first 10 overs. From those deliveries he scored 15 out of a total of 36 runs made by himself and Barber. As if that were not enough, Boycott made things worse by calling for a suicidal single off the last ball of the eleventh over which would have given him the bowling yet again. So crazily, stupidly, Bob Barber was run out. It had happened too many times during his career and supported the view that Boycott was selfish.

For many of Boycott's partners it was no joking matter either. Randall (during Boycott's Trent Bridge comeback), Gooch (when on 99 in a Test Match) and many others all had cause for regret. But the Barber incident was the prelude to a generally disappointing tour for Boycott, particularly at the latter end of the trip. After Australia, New Zealand did not hold out the prospect of any improvement in his personal fortunes.

Averages for 1965–66 Series v Australia

Tests	I	NO	Runs	HS	Avge
5	9	2	300	84	42.85

Bowling: 23–4–89–2   **Centuries:** 0
Fielding: 1   **Half-Centuries:** 3

Cumulative Test Career Averages

Tests	I	NO	Runs	HS	Avge
18	31	5	1,121	117	43.11

Bowling: 111–30–309–7   **Centuries:** 2
Fielding: 3   **Half-Centuries:** 7

Three Tests were scheduled for New Zealand. Boycott played in the first two games (both drawn), making 13 runs in three innings and, to top a miserable conclusion to the tour, was dropped for the third Test. Of the two games in which he took part the first Test, at Christchurch, was exceptional. Boycott scored 4 in each innings but the real action came in a startling New Zealand second innings. Requiring 197 to win in two hours twenty minutes, Higgs (9–7–5–4), Brown (4–2–6–1) and Parfitt (6–3–5–2) reduced the Kiwis to 22 for 7. They were in grave danger of beating their own unenviable lowest-ever Test score of 26 all out, also made against England, but Pollard and Cunis succeeded in batting through the final thirty-five minutes to take New Zealand to 48 for 8 at the close.

At Dunedin, Boycott failed again. He was bowled by Bartlett for 5 in his one innings but there was a mitigating factor in Boycott's favour.

Bartlett possessed an action that was a combination of Charlie Griffith and Geoff Griffin and it produced a result much worse. Consequently, Bartlett was diplomatically dropped for the last Test as was Boycott for reasons of form. In fact, there had been a possibility of him being made twelfth man for the second Test. It was to have been either him or Brown because the selectors wanted to give Barry Knight a run in the Test team. As Boycott had not missed a game on the tour since mid-January he was in need of a break but, with Brown suffering from a slight strain, he had to play at Dunedin.

Boycott took two catches in the NZ first innings but the chance he dropped at deep mid-on took away the gilt even from that pleasure. The big-hitting Dick Motz slammed five fours and three sixes in a whirlwind knock of 57 but it was due mainly to his good luck in being dropped by Boycott off a chest-high chance early in his innings. What had begun so well for Boycott in December with consecutive Test scores of 45, 68* and 51 against Australia ended badly in March against the New Zealanders.

A brief announcement in *The Times* seemed to sum it up:

'G. Boycott, the Yorkshire opening bat, who had looked stale and out of touch since leaving Australia, has been dropped to make room for Brown, who was kept out of the second Test by injury.'

Averages for 1965–66 Series v New Zealand

Tests	I	NO	Runs	HS	Avge
2	3	0	13	5	4.33

Bowling: 12–6–30–0   **Centuries:** 0
Fielding: 2   **Half-Centuries:** 0

Cumulative Test Career Averages

Tests	I	NO	Runs	HS	Avge
20	34	5	1,134	117	39.10

Bowling: 123–36–339–7   **Centuries:** 2
Fielding: 5   **Half-Centuries:** 7

4 Indian stunner, West Indies summer

1966 proved to be a swings and roundabouts season for Boycott. Generally, the picture was good; 1,854 runs in all first-class matches, average 39.44, was not only 400 runs more than in 1965 but his six centuries were an enormous improvement on his previous season. However, where it mattered most of all, in the Test Matches, the series against the West Indies was disappointing for him. Less than 200 runs from four tests, 186 at 26.57, was not par for his course. In mitigation it should be said that 1966 was the fifth consecutive season of top-grade continuous playing, summer and winter, that Boycott had undertaken since the summer of 1964.

Towards the end of the 1965–6 Australasian tour Boycott had been reported, as *The Times* had said, as looking stale. Perhaps it was as well that there was no official Test tour planned for the winter of 1966–7, for on figures alone Boycott seemed to have played a surfeit of cricket and needed time to recharge his batteries. A winter away from the sport was the ideal antidote. In the meantime, however, there was the 1966 home season to negotiate.

It began well enough with a knock of 123 against the MCC for Yorkshire at Lord's in April but he did not make another three figure score until June when Warwickshire suffered to the tune of 136 not out at Edgbaston. The lull did not pass unnoticed. It was deemed by the England selectors to be sufficient grounds for leaving Boycott out of the side for the first Test against the West Indies. With Boycott's omission from the third Test in New Zealand, it was the second successive Test he had missed.

Eric Russell was the player picked ahead of Boycott (and Edrich) to partner the new recruit, Colin Milburn, since Russell was in better current form than either Boycott or Edrich but Boycott returned for the second Test, ready to form a new opening partnership with the boisterous Milburn who was being hailed as the new big-hitting hope of English cricket.

Potentially, the union could have been as explosive as the pairing of Boycott and Bob Barber. The twin temperaments of Milburn and Barber were very similar, both believed in putting bat to ball in a vigorous manner. With Boycott providing the ideal foil to either of them the situation seemed perfect, in theory at least. Sadly, the Boycott–Milburn partnership never achieved the success of the Boycott–Barber pairing. It does not belittle Milburn in any way to categorise Barber as the more polished, accomplished performer. Milburn, by his own admission, was a hitter. Barber's more stylish technique, coupled with similar enterprise accounted for his greater success with Boycott.

Whatever the outcome, the strategem of combining Boycott with Milburn was put to the test, literally, at Lord's, but rain curtailed play to two-and-three-quarter hours on the first day and the West Indies could advance only as far as 156 for 4. Shortly after lunch on the second day they were all out for 269, the last 4 wickets fell after lunch for 22 runs. Into the fray stepped Boycott and Milburn but the Durham half of the partnership quickly went with the score at 8. In his place Boycott found a ready ally in Tom Graveney who was playing in his first Test for three years. The pair added 115 runs for the second wicket, the first of only two century partnerships they shared together in Tests, and which lasted until shortly before the close of play. Boycott was the batsman out, being caught by Griffith off Lance Gibbs for 60.

England, due principally to Graveney (96) and Parks (91) gained a first innings lead of 86 runs. That lead took on a positively winning hue when, forty minutes prior to lunch on the fourth morning, the West Indies lost their fifth wicket at 95. Their hopes were apparently dashed; no more than 9 runs ahead with half the side out. However, at that juncture two cousins joined forces in the type of Test Match partnership that occurs but rarely. Garfield Sobers (163*) and David Holford (105*), better known as a leg-spinner, put on 274 runs together and took away from England a seemingly certain victory. Sobers did not declare his record-breaking sixth wicket stand (in England–West Indies Tests) closed until forty minutes before lunch on the last day, thus setting England 284 runs to win in four hours. Rain washed away one of those hours and a draw became inevitable. It gave Boycott little opportunity to shine in the time remaining.

In fact, the highlight of the last day came after Boycott had been caught behind the wicket off Griffith for 25. Milburn, at his belligerent best, slammed 126* to add to a similar type of innings, of 94, that he had played in the first Test at Old Trafford. The innings at Lord's did not take England to victory but it served as a wonderful tonic against opponents who were, generally, a class above them. In what was a depressing summer (the series was lost 3–1) Milburn was one of the few bright lights to shine but, as if to emphasise the swings and roundabouts of this 1966 season, Boycott himself shone just as brightly in the third Test at Trent Bridge, and that despite scoring a 'duck' in the first innings!

The West Indies won the game by 139 runs but Boycott played his best Test of the whole summer. Once more England took a healthy first innings advantage of 90 runs but in the self-same fashion as that at Lord's, allowed the West Indies to bat their way back into the game. The West Indies had batted first, totalling 235 and that was more than they deserved, for England's fielding was abysmal. Significantly, Boycott alone was praised for his work in the field but while his team-mates were extremely poor in the first innings they were to be even worse in the second.

Everything began to run away from England after they had made a satisfactory 325 all out. The West Indies began batting again on the third day, and at close of play were 138 for 2, but subsequently the action centred almost exclusively on Basil Butcher. In addition to scoring 209*, he had the rare distinction of sharing in three successive century partnerships in a Test innings (a feat which Boycott himself was to emulate the following year); but Butcher was dropped no less than *five* times. Similarly benefited were the third, fourth and fifth wicket partnerships of 110 with Kanhai, 107 with Nurse and 173 with Sobers, respectively. Thus was Sobers enabled to declare late on the fourth day, offering to England a target of 393 runs for victory.

In the final minutes of the fourth day England were taken to 30 without loss by Boycott and Milburn, and on the last morning the innings was enhanced by a superb display of Boycott's skill and defensive technique. There had been criticism in the past, there would assuredly be more in the future for this type of batting, but at Trent Bridge there could be no carping at Boycott's tactics. The fifth ball of the first over of the day had dispatched Milburn and with wickets continuing to fall steadily right through the morning session Boycott played a lone hand in defying the West Indies.

Unfortunately, Boycott also was one of the pre-lunch victims. He fell immediately before the adjournment to a catch by Sobers off Griffith but his innings had been a gem, a marvellous cameo performance amongst fellow actors who allowed their contributions to disintegrate. Nor was Boycott all stolid defence. His 71 included six boundaries together with a powerfully pulled six off Sobers. Tempered aggression was delightfully mixed with resolute caution, but D'Oliveira (54) alone copied his example in offering further resistance before England stumbled to 253 all out, and defeat by 130 runs.

Boycott did not gain any further scores of substance in the series. In the two remaining Tests he totalled 30 runs (12, 14 and 4) although in the final match, under the new captaincy of Brian Close, England succeeded in salvaging some damaged pride by defeating the West Indies by an innings. Nottingham was Boycott's one moment of glory in the series, which was generally a huge disappointment to England's and Boycott's followers alike.

Furthermore, although it was still some way in the future, some dark clouds were gathering for Boycott; clouds which presaged much more trouble than a mere run of low scores. For the first time in his career serious controversy was looming for Boycott and, sadly, a pattern was to be set for the rest of his career. From 1967 onwards Boycott and controversy would advance together along a career path which unfortunately would never again be centred on cricket alone.

Averages for 1966 Series v West Indies

Tests	I	NO	Runs	HS	Avge
4	7	0	186	71	26.57

Bowling: **Centuries:** 0
Fielding: 0   **Half-Centuries:** 2

Cumulative Test Career Averages

Tests	I	NO	Runs	HS	Avge
24	41	5	1,320	117	36.66

Bowling: 123–36–339–7   **Centuries:** 2
Fielding: 5   **Half-Centuries:** 9

Whatever lay in the future, and despite his lack-lustre Test displays, Boycott had still been able to reap a sizeable harvest in 1966, particularly at the expense of Nottinghamshire who, in a county fixture played at Sheffield in July, were given extra-special Boycott treatment in the shape of a century in each innings, 103 and 105, the first occasion on which he had performed the feat in first-class cricket. It would not be the last such feat against Nottinghamshire for there would be another twin-century match in 1983 and, over his whole career, Boycott was to favour Nottinghamshire with more centuries than any other opposing team. At Test level, however, the twin-hundred feat was one of the few achievements to elude Boycott, although he could not have gone closer when he made 99 and 112 at Port-of-Spain on England's 1973–4 tour of the West Indies.

Boycott was finally successful against the 1966 Caribbean side when he scored 131 against them for T. N. Pearce's XI in an end-of-season festival game at Scarborough. It was far removed from the earlier mid-summer battles in the Test arena but after the disappointments of the four games in the full series, the final festival century surely tasted sweet to him. Also to follow was the winter 1966–7, during which he would not play a single game of first-class cricket. After playing in 109 first-class fixtures from April 1964 to September 1966 it was a break that he very much needed.

On Monday 19 June 1967 a headline in *The Times* announced:
BOYCOTT MADE TO PAY PENALTY
In the correspondent's words that followed, Boycott had been 'sent into a corner'; he had in fact been sacked from the England team after scoring 246 not out against India in the first Test of that summer. If there

was any irony at all in the situation it came from the fact that Boycott's career-best Test score was made at Headingley, the Yorkshire headquarters; but, by any reckoning, that was the sole mitigating factor in Boycott's favour, for his innings was played against an attack that would have hardly tested a good League side. The innings was hugely boring. It was boring not only to the Yorkshire fans on the ground but also to the millions of watching television viewers who simply could not understand how a batsman of Boycott's skill and calibre could allow himself to be so stifled and to be so very stifling.

The heart of the issue centred on the first day's play of the Headingley Test. England reached 281 for 3 but Boycott's share of that total, made in a full *six* hours play, was only 106*. Seventeen runs an hour off a lightweight Indian attack that was sub-Test Match standard! There was little to say in his defence.

As was often the case with Boycott the wound was self-inflicted. The lack of a serious challenge to the English batsmen from the Indians was apparent to all and sundry. In the full series of three Tests, England won every game with consummate ease; the Indians were so weak that, without their captain M. A. K. Pataudi they would hardly have made any show at all. So thin were their resources that in the third Test, half of their opening attack was the *reserve* wicketkeeper B. K. Kunderan. Consequently, Boycott's ultra-cautious lack of enterprise and originality drew the all-round condemnation it deserved. The selectors awarded him, in effect, a one-match ban.

For the statistician, the innings produced all manner of records for Boycott. Firstly, 246 not out was the highest first-class score of his career to date; it was also the highest Test score he would achieve in his England career of 108 matches; it was the highest individual innings in Anglo–Indian Tests and, whilst those records were being set, Boycott shared his largest partnership for any wicket in all his 193 Test innings. That was a fourth wicket stand of 252 runs made with Basil D'Oliveira (109), which ended only 14 runs short of the all-time record for England–India matches created by W. R. Hammond and T. S. Worthington at the Oval in 1936, that too being for the fourth wicket. Prior to that record, and also part of it, Boycott achieved the unusual Test Match distinction of taking part in three consecutive century partnerships: first 139 for the second wicket with Ken Barrington (93), second 107 for the third wicket with Tom Graveney (59) plus the fourth wicket stand with D'Oliveira. But as thousands of cricket followers said: 'What a way to do it!'

A measure of Boycott's slowness can be gleaned from the proceedings on the second day during the three-and-a-half hours further batting allowed by skipper Brian Close. Boycott advanced his score in that period by some 140 runs. Therefore, in what amounted to little more than half of the playing time of the previous day Boycott doubled his score and added another 34 runs. Worse followed for Boycott. While fielding in the Indian first innings he trod on the ball and could not field again until the fifth day. Then he did not bat when England required only 125 runs for victory.

Boycott returned to the team for the third Test at Birmingham, when the Indians' cup of woe was full to overflowing. Nevertheless, for a variety of reasons, the game proved to be one of the most interesting Tests that Boycott played in for England. With Guha, Mohol and Rusi Surti all injured, the reserve wicketkeeper Budhi Kunderan had to open the bowling with Subramanya. However, of much more interest from a bowling point of view, was that all but one of the English wickets to fall in the game went to India's world-renowned quartet of spin bowlers. That in itself was quite remarkable, for the third Test at Edgbaston in 1967 was the *only* occasion in their entire, and largely parallel, careers that Bedi, Chandrasekhar, Prasanna and Venkataraghavan all played together in the same Test side for India.

Although England won a low-scoring game comfortably by 132 runs with two days to spare (20 wickets fell on the second day) Boycott had a less than happy time. In the first innings he was stumped, for 25, for the first time in his Test career, by Engineer off Bedi, and in the second innings he was clean bowled by Subramanya, the one English wicket to fall that did not go to an Indian spinner. Subra – who? one might ask. Between 1965 and 1968, Subramanya played in nine Test Matches for India against England, Australia, the West Indies and New Zealand and from these nine appearances he took 3 Test wickets. G. T. Dowling and V. Pollard from New Zealand provided two but the prize he could treasure most was:

G. BOYCOTT   b. SUBRAMANYA   6

As some consolation, Boycott held two catches in India's second innings, the second one being a brilliant diving effort right in front of the sight screen to clinch the game for England. The Test was over but what a strange game it had been! It was completed in less than three days, 20 wickets fell in a single day, India's four famed spinners played together for the one and only time in a Test, two wicketkeepers (Engineer and Kunderan) opened the batting for India, Kunderan then opened the bowling. Finally, Boycott was dismissed by an almost unknown bowler!

Averages for 1967 Series v India

Tests	I	NO	Runs	HS	Avge
2	3	1	277	246*	138.50

Bowling: **Centuries:** 1

Fielding: 2   **Half-Centuries:** 0

Cumulative Test Career Averages

Tests	I	NO	Runs	HS	Avge
26	44	6	1,597	246*	42.02

Bowling: 123–36–339–7   **Centuries:** 3

Fielding: 7   **Half-Centuries:** 9

As India seemed to retreat, so Pakistan advanced, and they were the second visitors that summer. For varying reasons Boycott played only in the middle game of the three-match series. It was another reminder that, despite finishing third in the national averages, the season was a difficult, exasperating time for Boycott. He missed the first Test against Pakistan because his father died. He played in the second Test at Trent Bridge (15 and 1* in a 10-wicket victory) but had to drop out of the third Test with a throat infection almost as the game was due to start.

Domestically, the season was little better. Thirteen scores of more than 50 could not be turned into centuries and, apart from the Indian double hundred and a century against the Pakistanis for Yorkshire, there were only two similar scores in the County Championship. These were 102 versus Glamorgan and 220* versus Northamptonshire, all of which were made in Yorkshire. However, Boycott's dogged perseverance showed through with his total of 1,910 first-class runs and in the immediate future there was a promise of much better things to come with his first tour of the Caribbean during the winter of 1967–8 with the MCC. Indeed, with typical resilience, Boycott was to play a tour that positively sparkled with individual brilliance. How swiftly the fortunes of cricket can change!

Averages for 1967 Series v Pakistan

Tests	I	NO	Runs	HS	Avge
1	2	1	16	15	16.00

Cumulative Test Career Averages

Tests	I	NO	Runs	HS	Avge
27	46	7	1,613	246*	41.36

Bowling: 123–36–339–7   **Centuries:** 3

Fielding: 7   **Half-Centuries:** 9

By the time Boycott made his first trip to the Caribbean in the early new year of 1968 he was a well-established member of the England team. His twenty-seven Tests had encompassed the whole range of Test-playing opposition and 1,600 runs from those games had produced a healthy 40-plus average. Yet, it was not until Boycott went to the West Indies that he realised his full potential in every sense and dominated the opposition from the crease in a fashion that he had previously threatened but only rarely, as in the Gillette Cup Final of 1965, achieved.

Now, from sixteen innings in the eleven first-class matches in which he played, Boycott scored 1,154 runs at an average of 82.42. Such was his consistency on the tour that only six of those sixteen visits to the crease failed to produce at least a half-century. He began with 135 in the opening first-class fixture, against the President's XI, and ended with 116 in the first innings of the fifth Test, the last game on the schedule. Altogether he made six half-centuries and four hundreds (243, 165, 135 and 116) on the tour. During one spell mid-way through, three consecutive innings produced an amazing 498 runs for Boycott and his team. After 165 against the Leeward Islands, he followed with 243 against the strong Barbados side and then hit 90 off the full West Indies Test attack in his one innings of the drawn third Test.

Boycott was virtually irrepressible on the tour but his best innings was probably the 80* he made in the second innings of the fourth Test. Victory there gave England both the match and the series (by 1–0) and nobody played a bigger role than Boycott. That 80* was decisive. Furthermore, it was an ideal reply to critics who repeatedly alleged that he batted slowly. For Boycott timed his innings with precision to take England home with three minutes and no more than eight deliveries to spare. In England's cause that performance was worth half-a-dozen double hundreds against Barbados or any other Island team.

In addition, Boycott had made much the same impression when the Test series began. At Port-of-Spain in the first Test, Wesley Hall suffered the unusual indignity of being struck for four boundaries in his first 2 overs by Boycott. Critics with short memories should take note of that. When Lillee and Thomson were firing all kinds of flack at England in the early 1970s it was said that Boycott 'ducked out' of facing the Australian 'terrors'. Whatever the reasons were for his self-imposed exile it was hardly likely to be fear. Boycott had faced the equals, in speed, of Lillee and Thomson in the shape of Wes Hall and Charlie Griffith. In fact, Hall was probably the fastest of the four and, more to Boycott's credit, he had taken large scores off Hall and Griffith. It seems unlikely, therefore, that having faced these opponents, Boycott would be frightened by Lillee and Thomson.

In the first Test England very nearly beat the West Indies after forcing them to follow-on some 205 runs adrift of their mammoth first innings total of 568 all out. Boycott's share, including his hammering of Hall, was 68 while the main bulk of the scoring was made by Barrington (143) and Graveney (118). As it was not until well into the fourth day before the West Indies began their follow-on, an English victory appeared to be unlikely and this was apparently confirmed by careful batting from Nurse (42), Camacho (43), Kanhai (37) and Butcher (52) which took the West Indies to 164 for 2 by mid-afternoon of the last day. The game seemed as good as saved but the fall of Kanhai to Robin Hobbs began a sensational collapse. In the last over before tea David Brown fired out

Butcher, Deryck Murray and Griffith and from 164 for 2 the West Indies had crashed to 180 for 8.

The loss of 6 wickets in an hour gave England a double opportunity for victory. They could either win by an innings or, at worst, would have only a miniscule number of runs to make to win once the last 2 West Indian wickets had been claimed. Unfortunately the indefatigable Sobers (33*) and Hall proceeded to bat right through the final session of the match. What would have transpired if Boycott had held on to a chance from Hall, off the bowling of Brown, immediately after tea is a matter of endless speculation but scant blame could be attached to Boycott for he was fielding at *short-leg*, which was not Boycott's favourite let alone usual position.

At Kingston, where the second Test was staged, it was England's turn to cling on to a draw by the skin of their teeth. The game suffered a particularly bad riot which resulted in the lost time being made up on an unscheduled sixth day. For Boycott, Kingston was his one 'miss' of the tour. He made 17 and 0, bowled by Hall and Sobers respectively, but it was the last occasion on the tour when the West Indian bowlers gained the upper hand. Neither at Bridgetown, or Port-of-Spain again, or Georgetown would he be dismissed as cheaply.

A rain-shortened first day and painfully slow batting by Steve Camacho at Bridgetown set the tone of the third Test. Camacho made 33* in a first day reduced to ten minutes less than four hours. He eventually made 57 off 81 overs; and people in England complained about Boycott batting slowly! When he and Edrich finally got to the crease, in the middle of the third morning, they were so much in unison with each other that they put together the highest partnership, 172, of any of the thirty-five innings that they opened for England. Boycott got to within 10 runs of his hundred before being first out, leg-before to Sobers; it was the first of the few occasions when, having reached the nineties, he did not go on to make a century. In fact it would happen on only five more occasions, thus making six scores between 90 and 99 in his 193 Test innings.

The first wicket stand went a long way towards giving England a slender 100-run lead but with little more than a full day's play remaining when the West Indies began to bat a second time the fate of the match had already been decided. It was the one game of the entire series which did not have an exciting climax. The West Indies batted out time to reach 284 for 6.

Three successive draws, however, did not mean that the series was dull. Two of the matches could easily have gone to either side, but the deadlock was finally ended when the teams returned to Port-of-Spain for the fourth Test where the West Indies batted first and scored 526 for 7 declared. Boycott and Edrich were undaunted by the challenge. They began their reply with 86 for the first wicket, at which point Edrich was out, and Boycott followed at 112 with 62 to his name. Then Cowdrey played a marvellous innings of 148 to hold England together. There was a middle order collapse but a Kentish partnership of 113 for the sixth wicket between Cowdrey and the youthful Alan Knott (69*), at three an over, was a superb response to the West Indies. The pair not only saved the follow-on but were batting so comfortably that England appeared to be completely safe from defeat, until, that is, Cowdrey was rather dubiously given out caught behind off Butcher. Ironically, it was this doubtful decision, which could have ruined England, that made a definite result possible.

Basil Butcher was no more than a very occasional Test bowler but he produced some remarkable figures from a 14 over, rain-interrupted spell which possibly influenced Sobers into thinking that England were vulnerable to spin. Butcher's figures were 4 wickets in 3 overs, 5 for 15 in 10 overs and he ended the innings with figures of 14–4–34–5. Consequently, Sobers declared the West Indies second innings closed at 92 for 2 to set England the generous target of 215 runs to win in two-and-three-quarter hours.

With a good start of 55 in 19 overs from the ever-dependable Boycott and Edrich the chase began. After Edrich was out a quiet spell ensued but after tea Cowdrey (71) cut loose with a vengeance, hotly pursued by Boycott. From 18 overs 100 runs were plundered, the score rising from 73 to 173, and in total they added 118 for the second wicket before Cowdrey (who batted for just seventy-six minutes) was caught by Sobers off Gibbs. Ten runs later, at 183, Graveney was bowled by Gibbs for 2 but at that juncture Boycott took complete control of the situation.

At the earlier dismissal of Cowdrey, 42 runs had still been required with thirty-five minutes remaining. Within seventeen minutes of losing Graveney the 200 total had been raised by Boycott, who hit Gibbs for two boundaries in one over to reach the mark. Fifteen minutes and 4 overs later, England had won with a bare three minutes remaining. Boycott's 80* had paced the innings to perfection, especially in conjunction with Cowdrey, and England had taken a decisive, if unexpected, lead in the series.

No less exciting was the final Test at Georgetown. Sobers (152) and Kanhai (150) dominated the early play, putting on 250 for the fourth wicket and between them scoring all but 112 runs of the West Indies total of 414 all out. To this, Boycott replied admirably with 116, the highest Test score he was to make in three tours of the West Indies, and with Cowdrey he added 172 for the second wicket, of which Cowdrey's share was only 59 runs. Then the England middle order collapsed in its usual fashion but into the breach stepped an unlikely saviour. Tony Lock, specially flown in to replace the injured Titmus, slammed 89 runs in a stand of 109 for the ninth wicket with Pat Pocock which took up the last one hundred minutes of the fourth day and early part of the final morning. Pocock's role was purely passive for, quite the opposite of Lock, he took eighty-two minutes to score his first run!

England were bowled out for 371 and Sobers was once again in regal form when his team batted again. He would undoubtedly have collected his second century of the match but at 95 he ran out of partners. His brilliant innings had taken the West Indies to 264 all out which offered England the improbable target of scoring 308 runs to win or the no less arduous task of batting for all of the last day in order to save the game. The former was never feasible for Gibbs intervened to shatter the England innings, all in the space of ninety-five minutes, and from that setback it was almost miraculous that England survived to gain a draw.

First, Gibbs caught Edrich off the bowling of Sobers, 33 for 1. He struck next to remove both Barrington and Graveney for 'ducks' and at 39 caught D'Oliveira off his own bowling (39 for 4). All the while Boycott had remained rock-like and totally secure but Gibbs was far from being a spent force. He penetrated Boycott's usually impregnable defences to bowl him for 30, 41 for 5 wickets. Once again the men of Kent, Cowdrey (82) and Knott (73*) stepped forward to rescue England. They patiently added 127 for the sixth wicket until Cowdrey fell leg-before-wicket to Gibbs. There were then seventy minutes playing time remaining but nothing could move Knott. He was still at the crease after four hours and ingeniously contrived sufficient tail-end support to save the game for England. It was a great effort by a player who, at that time, was still very much a novice at Test level.

When Pocock was given out off a first-bounce catch Knott's work could have been doomed to failure, yet the left-arm pace bowler Jeff Jones summoned enough batting skill to survive the last over trom Gibbs and with that nerve-wracking performance over, the rubber belonged to England. Gibbs, however, was also a hero. His extraordinary figures, 40–20–60–6, were testimony enough to the world-class performance he turned in and which so very nearly span the West Indies to victory in that final Test.

A thrilling tour, for both Boycott and England, thus ended on yet another note of high drama. Boycott's virtuoso performance had continued virtually non-stop from January through the first week of April when the tour ended. He had produced an unending stream of high-class batting and, in the process, excelled himself consistently in England's colours as he had never done previously. There was also the added satisfaction that, when he had scored 70 of his last Test century, he had reached the personal milestone of 2,000 Test runs. The first 1,000 runs had been raised in his sixteenth Test; not unusually for Boycott, the second 1,000 took exactly the same number of Tests, being realised in his thirty-second match for England. That Boycott trait, his hallmark, of consistency was beginning to show itself more and more as his career progressed.

5 Missed Tests and West Indies again

The back trouble that Boycott had suffered in the early stages of the 1965–6 Australasian tour flared up again during the 1968 season. Whereas in Australia it had kept Boycott out of the opening fixtures of the tour, this later attack was much more serious. It removed him from cricket completely from mid-July until the beginning of September. Boycott missed in the process the fourth and fifth Test Matches plus numerous important games for Yorkshire. For Boycott the break could not have occurred at a worse time. When the period of inactivity began he had struck a rich seam of run-scoring that could have taken him on to his highest tally for Yorkshire since his debut.

Beginning in May, Boycott went on a run-making rampage. One hundred against Sussex was followed by 132 versus Leicestershire, 180* against Warwickshire and 125 off Gloucestershire. That was four centuries in less than a month and he complemented them with a fifth in June, hitting a further 114 against Leicestershire. Then came the disastrous back injury. Not until 4 September could Boycott return to first-class cricket, in a Scarborough Festival game for an England XI against a Rest Of The World XI. Even after so many weeks without match practice his reappearance was as stunning as the start of the season had been. Scores of 93 and 115 made it look as if he had never been away. Boycott had lost none of his zest or appetite for runs, and to emphasise the point he made another unbeaten century, 102*, for Yorkshire versus MCC a week later, also at the Scarborough Festival.

From little more than half a season's work, Boycott finished top of the national first-class averages with 1,487 runs from thirty innings at 64.65 per innings. In the County Championship his average was even better; 77.40 for 774 runs scored from just fifteen innings. The five centuries for Yorkshire in the championship by the middle of June together with his two at the Scarborough Festival make it pleasurable to speculate as to what heights Boycott would have scaled in 1968 had he been able to play the full season. Not only was his form electrifying in the early part of the season; it was little impaired, if at all, when he returned at Scarborough.

On the other side of the coin, in the three internationals in which he took part Boycott was much less effective than in the domestic game. The first Test, at Old Trafford, was lost by 159 runs and the second and third matches were drawn with Boycott's highest score in his five innings being 49. At Manchester he batted twice, making 35 and 11, but his best moment came in the field when he assisted in running out Ian Chappell. Paul Sheahan had played the ball towards Boycott at cover and immediately set off for a run. Chappell had little chance of making his ground despite Boycott's return to Knott being wide. The Kent wicket-keeper still had time to run in five yards with the ball in his gloves and break the wicket with Chappell well stranded in the middle of the pitch. Nonetheless, and despite losing their last 6 wickets for 38 runs, Australia still reached 357 all out in their first innings.

Boycott and Edrich began their reply for England twenty-five minutes before lunch on the second morning. In that short period they made 5 runs and in an afternoon of continuous interruptions put 60 on the board before the weather finally won the major battle of the day at 5.15pm. Two hours in all were lost for rain and bad light. Under such trying circumstances Boycott and Edrich performed exceptionally well in keeping their concentration and their partnership intact and on the third morning they advanced further, taking the score to 86. At that juncture there was a run-out; however, on this occasion it was not the fault of Boycott. Edrich called and went for a third run only for Walters' long, fast, accurate return from the deep to beat him to the wicket. It was not so much bad judgement as extremely good fielding by Walters; it also gave the game to Australia.

From 86 for 0 England crumbled to 144 for 9 wickets. Had it not been for a last-ditch effort by Snow and Pocock, with 21 runs for the tenth wicket, Australia would have most certainly enforced the follow-on. As it was their lead of 192 runs made it difficult to envisage defeat for them especially when their lead was extended by another 60 runs up by the close of play on the third day. On the Monday, Walters crowned a fine all-round performance with his second 80 of the game. Barry Jarman hit lustily for 41 and Australia's 220 all out gave England the daunting options of making 413 runs for victory or batting for nine-and-a-quarter hours to secure a draw.

Neither option seemed remotely possible although defeat did not appear to figure in Boycott's thoughts when he opened England's second innings. He attempted to force the pace right from the start, scoring 11 out of 13. McKenzie induced the edged shot, Redpath took the catch in the slips, and Boycott returned to the pavilion, as did the rest of his team-mates at regular intervals. Barber (46) and D'Oliveira (87*) were the sole batsmen to survive for any length of time, their sixth-wicket stand of 80 runs taking the match into the fifth day, but Australia still remained well in control. Once Barber and D'Oliveira were parted the end of the innings came rapidly and gave Australia a comfortable victory by 159 runs.

From Manchester the Test Match circus moved on to Lord's where

Boycott made his best score of the series, 49, in what was the 200th Test encounter between England and Australia. Disappointingly, what should have been a showpiece occasion was ruined because rain took away half of the playing time. Still more depressing was the loss of a winning opportunity when Australia were shot out for just 78 runs after England had made 351 for 7 wickets declared. A golden chance of squaring the series had been washed away.

At the start of the match, the pitch was very lively, even nasty at times, and in the eighty-three minutes of play possible on the first day England laboured uncomfortably to 53 for the loss of 1 wicket. Boycott lost Edrich with 10 runs on the board but found a willing replacement in Milburn who stayed with him until well into the second day as they added 132 runs. Against difficult, often short-pitched, bowling on a wicket that gave considerable help to the bowlers they batted with commendable skill. Boycott was ever watchful, while Milburn countered McKenzie by pulling him for six but, in return, was hit several times on the body by wickedly rising deliveries. Nonetheless, they stuck to their task until McKenzie once again had Boycott snapped up, this time by Sheahan. Play was in stark contrast to the much-shortened first day and only fifteen minutes time was lost while England reached 314 for 5 at the end of the second day. Then the rain came again. Less than 14 overs could be bowled in three short spells on day three. Despite the dramatic Australian dismissal for 78, the possibility of a definite result was precluded by the weather.

England declared at their overnight third-day position of 351 for 7, and with the aid of some exceptional close catching, promptly routed Australia in the first innings. Cowdrey, in particular, was outstanding. He held three catches to pass W. R. Hammond's world test record of 110 catches. Following on, the Australians fared a lot better. They made 50 without loss by the end of the fourth day and that, in effect, was the end of the match. Play could not begin until mid-afternoon on the last day, when only two-and-a-half hours remained. By tea, Lawry was the one batsman dismissed and although Redpath, Cowper and Walters all fell after the interval, Paul Sheahan kept Ian Chappell company for fifty minutes without scoring a run and avoided any danger of defeat.

Edgbaston staged the third Test and, characteristically for 1968, there was no play at all possible on the first day. When the game did get under way Boycott was at the crease with Edrich. Since the England team contained only five specialist batsmen, neither opener was in a mood to take any risks. Consequently, the second day saw them proceed very cautiously and sedately to 65 without being parted. A further 15 runs were added after lunch at which juncture Boycott attempted to sweep the 'mystery' spinner Gleeson. He failed to make contact with the ball, but his proffered pad unfortunately did – 80–1–36. Although out, Boycott's work in the middle was far from finished. Colin Cowdrey, playing in his 100th Test, needed a runner and Boycott (a surprising but convenient choice) filled the role. Cowdrey's 104 not only took England towards a final score of 409 all out but also took Cowdrey past the personal milestone of 7,000 Test runs. After Hammond, he was only the second player in Test history up to that time to perform the feat. While Boycott was performing those services his own personal tally of Test runs amounted to 2,207, a long, long way behind Cowdrey. In fact, Boycott would achieve the same target in six Tests fewer than Cowdrey but that was not to be for another thirteen years.

Australia began batting on the third day. At the close their 109 for 1 was, to all intents and purposes, for two wickets because Lawry had had to retire hurt with a broken finger. At first he was not greatly missed. By lunch on the fourth day the total had risen to 193 for 4 but, in rapid succession, 5 wickets fell for 9 runs and at 222 all out Australia narrowly avoided the follow-on. Having to bat again England, therefore, went for quick runs to enable a declaration to be made that would leave sufficient time to bowl out Australia a second time. Boycott (31), Edrich (64) and Graveney (39*) all batted enterprisingly. Fifty-seven runs came for the first wicket followed by 74 for the second wicket and, twenty minutes before the close on the fourth day, Cowdrey was able to declare at 142 for 3, thus setting Australia 330 runs to win in six hours and ten minutes.

Cowper had to open with Redpath in place of the injured Lawry but the weather was determined to have the last say. In the odd ten minutes of the fourth day the makeshift opening pair made 9 runs from 3 overs and, although Redpath was trapped leg-before by Snow early on the last morning, he was to be England's solitary success of the day. Light drizzle turned to steady rain, which the batsmen endured for quarter-of-an-hour, until they had no option but to appeal against the downpour. The umpires stopped play at 12.30pm but it was not until three hours later that a final decision was taken to abandon the match. However, by that stage a draw was a foregone conclusion.

That Edgbaston Test, with Boycott's two innings in the thirties, proved to be his last really competitive match of the season. Not for the better part of a full year would he be back in a Test Match arena but, when that did occur, against the West Indies, he came back in dramatic style.

Averages for 1968 Series v Australia

Tests	I	NO	Runs	HS	Avge
3	5	0	162	49	32.40

Bowling: **Centuries:** 0

Fielding: 1   **Half-Centuries:** 0

Cumulative Test Career Averages

Tests	I	NO	Runs	HS	Avge
35	59	8	2,238	246*	43.89

Bowling: 123–36–339–7   **Centuries:** 4

Fielding: 9   **Half-Centuries:** 13

In addition to the last two Tests against Australia in 1968, Boycott also missed another three Test 'caps'. In the winter of 1968–9 a short three-Test tour of Pakistan was made by MCC under the captaincy of Colin Cowdrey. It was a hastily arranged affair, coming after a proposed tour of India was cancelled because the Indian Government could not release foreign exchange to back it up. However, apart from a few runs on his aggregate, Boycott missed little by staying at home, for the tour proved a fiasco. There were riots at every venue until the tour was aborted during the third Test when violence erupted yet again. That proved to be the last straw for the England management, although it was bad luck for Alan Knott who was 96* when the Test was abandoned. But maybe he did not greatly mind.

Boycott's refusal to go to either India or Pakistan (although he did eventually tour both countries with England) was another criticism he had to endure during his Test career. As characteristic of Boycott it was not a straightforward matter and there were valid points to be made on both sides. First and foremost, over the full eighteen years of his Test career, Boycott missed only *four* tours undertaken by England. In the years between his first and last tours, 1964–5 to 1981–2, MCC or England made fourteen official journeys abroad. During four winters, 1966–7, 1969–70, 1971–2 and 1975–6, there were no Test tours. Therefore, only in 1968–9 (to Pakistan), 1972–3 (to Indian and Pakistan), 1974–5 (to Australia and New Zealand) and 1976–7 (to Indian and Australia) did Boycott not tour. Furthermore, the two latter tours coincided with his three-year self-imposed exile from the England team when he played no Test cricket at home either. Consequently, only twice could it be fairly said that he refused to tour when the opportunity was available, compared to nine times when he did tour.

On the other hand, we shoud note the tours that Boycott did miss, particularly those to Asia. The reason given was that it was principally because he had his spleen removed as a child that he was loath to visit India or Pakistan. Immediately a difficult question arises, one on which the author sought medical opinion to try and discover how far the removal of a spleen might have an adverse effect upon a professional sporting adult in hot countries years after the operation. The opinion, in general terms, coupled with the fact that Boycott did go to both Pakistan and India on later, separate occasions, seems to indicate that, unless there were other related medical matters which were not disclosed at the time, the removal of the spleen would have virtually no ill-effect upon a person playing cricket in countries such as India or Pakistan. The spleen is an organ in the abdomen whose primary function is to make blood. Its removal from the body would not normally create a situation that would be exacerbated by the heat, dust or other discomforts usually endured in India or Pakistan. The conclusion to be drawn, therefore, seems clear, especially as Boycott went to both countries later in his career. However, any man has the right to choose which countries he will or will not visit and if Boycott did not want to go then he was entitled not to do so. Yet, when Boycott made his last England tour (to India!) he was only 230 runs away from the world test record of aggregate runs scored in a career.

The fact remains, however, that he did not go to Pakistan in 1968–9. When the 1969 home season dawned, the prospect was the joint opposition posed by the West Indies and New Zealand who would each play three Tests that summer against England. Strangely, by playing in all six Tests, it would be the very first occasion since his Test debut in 1964 that Boycott had participated in either a full Test series at home or a complete home programme in a single summer.

Prior to playing the three games against the West Indies, Boycott had taken part in seven separate home series for England, three consisting of five Tests and four of three Tests. Not once, even in the three-Test split-summer series, had he managed to appear throughout an entire campaign. Conversely, on each of his three main tours abroad (to South Africa, Australia and the West Indies) Boycott had played in every Test. However, such was Boycott's form in the first two Tests against the 1969 West Indians that only injury would have prevented him from fulfilling a complete home series for the first time. England too could claim two milestones: the 10-wicket victory gained in the first Test at Old Trafford was England's first win on that ground since 1959 and the first victory over the West Indies there since 1950.

The game was played as a heatwave commenced that was to last from June to November, but the extremely wet weather which prevailed throughout May had given batsmen scant opportunity to practise or to find their form. Therefore, England's first innings of 413 all out at Old Trafford took ten hours to complete because batsmen were forced to play with caution. Naturally Boycott was ideal for the situation. He batted for a shade more than five-and-a-half hours to register the highest of his five Test hundreds, 128, against the West Indies on a day in which England reached 261 for 3 wickets. There were two main partnerships, both passing the three-figure mark, with Edrich (58) and Graveney (75) keeping Boycott company.

The first wicket produced 112 runs but its closure was marred by yet another run-out. Boycott, facing Carew and requiring a single for his half century, drove the ball very straight and very hard back towards the bowler. He immediately called for a single but Carew had partly stopped the ball. Edrich, meanwhile, had answered the call. He set off, stopped and then started again only to be left high and dry when Clive Lloyd swooped on to the ball and returned it for the wicket to be broken.

Further drama followed after Boycott duly completed his 50 a few deliveries later. Hendriks, the West Indian wicketkeeper, standing well back to John Shepherd, dropped the simplest of catches off Boycott so that the Yorkshireman's excess profit of 78 runs was to cost the West Indies very dear. A third wicket partnership of 128 runs with Tom Graveney was another result. It lasted until less than half-an-hour from the close of play when Boycott finally succumbed after his valiant 128. On the second day the eventual course of the match was cast virtually in one session of play after England's innings closed at 413 all out.

The West Indies never recovered from losing Fredericks to the first ball of their innings, caught by Graveney off Snow. The collapse continued until on the stroke of 6.30, the West Indies were tottering on the brink of defeat with 104 for 6. After sixty-five minutes of play on the third morning the innings was over, at 147 all out. Illingworth was bound to enforce the follow-on.

At the second time of asking, chasing a deficit of 266 runs, the West Indies batted with far more relish. Only a tremendous slip catch by Phil Sharpe broke the first wicket partnership of 92 and at the end of the third day the West Indies had reached 215 for 4. On the rest day, Sunday, heavy thunderstorms began during the night. Heavy showers followed on the Monday and the fourth day was not merely severely shortened but gave the West Indies an added opportunity of saving the game. In the short time available for play they progressed to 258 for 7, just 8 runs in arrears, but on the last day only one hour was needed by England to complete the match. The last 3 wickets fell for 17 runs which left England 10 runs to win. Edrich started off with two boundaries and Boycott contributed a single.

At Lord's Boycott made another century. Not only Boycott, but Hampshire and Illingworth too, three Yorkshire centuries in the same Test. Jack Hampshire's effort was particularly meritorious for it was made on his Test debut. He was thus the first Englishman to perform that feat at Lord's. The West Indies, however, had been bowled out for 380 runs, the innings lasting until late into the second day. During this period of the game Boycott's quick reaction at square-leg ran out Sobers. The ball had rebounded towards him off Sobers' pads following which there was a misunderstanding between Sobers himself and Davis over the possibility of a leg-bye. Boycott bounded forward, scooped up the ball and continued running towards the stumps to whip-off the bails while Sobers stood helplessly out of his ground in the middle of the pitch.

It was not to be as good for Boycott when he opened England's first innings. England finished the second day at 46 for 4, with Boycott one of the victims, caught at the wicket off Shepherd for 23, and Edrich, Parfitt and D'Oliveira all failing to reach double figures. It was left to Hampshire (107), Illingworth (113), and Knott (53) to steer the English ship home to 344 all out, the innings closing early on the fourth day. The 36-run deficit was much less than appeared likely in the early stages of the innings.

The West Indies now batted into the final day before Sobers made a sporting declaration at 295 for 9 which set England to score 332 runs to win in five hours plus 20 overs. The time allowed was the sporting factor but the target seemed too high for England on the fifth day of a Test Match. Boycott took two-and-a-half hours over his first 50 runs. Peter Parfitt followed suit, spending two hours scoring 39 and a draw seemed to be the objective until Phil Sharpe enlivened proceedings. With Boycott, Sharpe (86) added 126 runs in ninety minutes but the change had come too late. Had they stayed together England might have won. In the event, they fell almost together, and 61 runs off the last 10 overs was too much to expect of the tail-end batsmen. Boycott hit sixteen boundaries in his innings of 106 before falling to a catch by Butcher off Shillingford; unfortunately, as far as Test Matches were concerned, the catch also signalled the end of any further significant influence by Boycott in the Test Matches of 1969. It was that kind of summer for him. From centuries to noughts in rapid succession.

The series ended at Headingley where England clinched the rubber 2–0 by virtue of an exciting victory by the narrow margin, in Test Match terms, of 30 runs but it was no happy homecoming for Boycott. His contribution was 12 and 0 and 'that dreaded cipher', as it has been quaintly described, was the prelude to an uncommonly bad run for him. The crest of 1969 had been Old Trafford and Lord's. The trough began at Headingley.

Averages for 1969 Series v West Indies

Tests	I	NO	Runs	HS	Avge
3	6	1	270	128	54.00

Bowling: **Centuries:** 2
Fielding: 0   **Half-Centuries:** 0

Cumulative Test Career Averages

Tests	I	NO	Runs	HS	Avge
38	65	9	2,508	246*	44.78

Bowling: 123–36–339–7   **Centuries:** 6
Fielding: 9   **Half-Centuries:** 13

When we consider that England trounced New Zealand 2–0 with consummate ease, it is surprising that Boycott should struggle, seemingly quite desperately at times, to score runs against the Kiwis. But his scores against them that summer were 0, 47, 0, 46, 8. In his forty-one Tests so far he had played against New Zealand seven times, batted on twelve occasions but on only one of these had he passed 50; that being his score of 76 in 1965 at Lord's. His performances against New Zealand, in fact, could hardly have been more at odds with his normal pattern for, up to and including 1969, half of his twelve innings, when facing their bowlers, had not even progressed beyond double figures. Of his total of 2,609 Test runs (after the New Zealand series) made at an average of 42.77, the varied New Zealand attacks had provided only 271 of those runs at an average of 24.64.

Averages for 1969 Series v New Zealand

Tests	I	NO	Runs	HS	Avge
3	5	0	101	47	20.20

Bowling: **Centuries:** 0
Fielding: 0   **Half-Centuries:** 0

Cumulative Test Career Averages

Tests	I	NO	Runs	HS	Avge
41	70	9	2,609	246*	42.77

Bowling: 123–36–339–7   **Centuries:** 6
Fielding: 9   **Half-Centuries:** 13

The second Test series of 1969 had run a remarkably parallel course to the trend of Boycott's domestic season. Only against the West Indies could it be termed successful by his own standards for, on top of the two Test centuries he made only one more first-class hundred. It came in a County Championship fixture at Headingley against Somerset: Boycott scored 105* but it made little overall impression on an aggregate of 1,283 runs made from thirty-nine first-class innings at an average of 38.87. While many a seasoned County professional might have been pleased with these returns, to Boycott they signified the lowest aggregate he had produced in any of his seven full seasons of first-class cricket. Such is the price of greatness. A fair season by any standards except his own.

Yet 1969 was not a disaster. The season ended on a high note when Yorkshire won the Gillette Cup for the second time. It was an occasion to be savoured. Not for another fourteen long years would Yorkshire win any honours, and when one did come, with the winning of the John Player Sunday League in 1983, it happened in the same year as Yorkshire finished bottom of the County Championship table for the first time in their history.

Significantly, as the 1960s faded and the 1970s began, so too a new era for Yorkshire was dawning, an era that seemed to revolve almost totally around Geoffrey Boycott. It would be a time of turmoil, trouble and strife that began in the early 1970s and festered for ten years or more, until it exploded in 1983. When Boycott took on the role of captain of Yorkshire in 1971 the era of the Boycott factions had arrived. The 'fors' and 'againsts' would, from that point onwards, draw up their battle lines. Yet it was a battle which could never be won by either side; the only loser was the Yorkshire County Cricket Club itself. Would Yorkshire cricket ever be the same again? Sadly, as entrenchment became the password, there would be no retreat by any of the rapidly appearing factions. It was a mess; everybody seemed to want their own way, everybody appeared blind to the pathway down which they were leading Yorkshire cricket. If the road to Hell is paved with good intentions, in Yorkshire they became overgrown by bigotry, self-centredness and craving for personal glory and power.

6 A glorious run of runs

Leaving aside the internal Yorkshire struggles that were slowly taking root within the County, Boycott's sixth Test of 1969 (the final game against New Zealand in August) was to be his last in that sphere for a considerable length of time. Fifteen months would elapse, practically to the day, before either he or England played another Test Match. The reasons for this were principally two-fold. In the first instance there was no official tour during the winter of 1969–70. That welcome break was followed by the summer in which the highly successful 'Stop The Tour' campaign was mounted to ensure that the planned tour by South Africa of England did not take place that year.

With no Test opposition available, a series of five 'Tests' was played by England against a hastily organised Rest of the World team but full Test Match status was not accorded to the series. Consequently Boycott, who played in two of the matches, and England missed official Test Match action from 26 August 1969 until 27 November 1970 when the opening Test of the 1970–1 tour of Australia began. It was a somewhat ironic situation for Boycott, missing a full Test series at home when he was both available, more than willing to participate and, more importantly, in prime form.

Boycott returned to domestic cricket in 1970 obviously refreshed by a winter's rest and immediately he began what was the outstanding scoring streak of his career. Indeed, the summer of 1970 marked the beginning of a regal supremacy which lasted sixteen months.

Taking into account the Australian tour between 1970 and 1971, Boycott had the equivalent of three complete, consecutive seasons of full-time cricket. Such consistency (surely not an over-employed expression in relation to the figures which will follow) and such overall control of every aspect of his batting was phenomenal. All pitches, bowlers, matches and circumstances seemed to come alike to Boycott to such an extent that in that period he scored an average of nearly 80 every time he went to the crease. The figures reveal the cresting of a wave that, even within Boycott's own prodigious career, was higher than all his previous achievements. From April 1970 until September 1971 he produced the following statistics from all his first-class appearances:

M	I	NO	Runs	HS	Avge	100's	50's	CT
58	94	16	6,089	260*	78.06	23	25	24

At first sight Boycott began in a rather sedate manner. He scored only four centuries during the 1970 season, but his full averages for that summer showed a vast improvement upon the previous year. The extra runs scored amounted to nearly 800; 2,051 runs at 55.43 compared to his 1969 total of 1,283 runs at 38.87 per innings. Of the centuries, two were of particular significance. The first came against Essex at Colchester in July when he scored 260* to surpass by 14 runs his previous highest first-class score. Following that Boycott scored 157 for an England side against the Rest of the World in the last match of that special series, at the Oval in August. Coming one before and one after those innings were scores of 148 against Kent at Sheffield, and 147* for another England team versus England's under-25s at the Scarborough Festival.

When the centuries were added to a dozen other scores of 50 or more it not only rounded off a very pleasing season but was also a heartening prelude to Boycott's second visit to Australia.

The Australian tour of 1970–1 confirmed Boycott's status as a great batsman. To many, this final seal of approval was hardly necessary, but a tour average of 95.93 runs per innings, from twelve first-class matches and twenty-two innings, was proof if anyone required it of great batsmanship. Boycott's tour figures show that in all first-class games he scored 1,535 runs including six centuries and seven half-centuries. In the Tests alone the five-match, ten-innings aggregate amounted to 657 runs at an average of 93.85 which was remarkably close to his overall average for the tour. Finally, there was further proof of Boycott's domination of the Australian Test attack in that, from those ten international innings, he scored 50 or more on seven occasions, and twice went on to make an unbeaten century.

There can be little doubt that only the injury which prevented Boycott from playing in the final Test of the series was also responsible for him not passing W. R. Hammond's record aggregate of 1,553 runs for an Australian tour, for Boycott's tally was a mere 18 runs short of the record when injury foreshortened his tour. However, cricket does not give up its records easily and, in any event, the number of Tests played in the series is worthy of mention. Eventually, the series stretched to an unprecedented *seven* matches but only after a change of itinerary which inserted a seventh Test into the programme after the third Test had been completely washed away. The extra game mattered little to England. Already leading 1–0 by that stage, and without both Boycott and Snow, they still won by 62 runs to take both the series and the Ashes. After fourteen years the Ashes were back with England. That, on top of his own considerable contribution, must have made Boycott feel on top of the world.

In fact, Geoff formed opening partnerships with Brian Luckhurst and then John Edrich which were the basic foundation upon which success could be wrought. They came to fruition under the astute captaincy of

Ray Illingworth who used his bowling resources, particularly John Snow, with the utmost skill. Four of the ten Test innings in which Boycott opened were given the boost of a century-plus start. Two were with Luckhurst and three, in consecutive innings, were with Edrich.

Boycott's own tour began with a score of 173 against South Australia in the opening match; he played in all four first-class fixtures up to the first Test at Brisbane. In addition to South Australia, both New South Wales (129*) and Queensland (124 retired hurt) also received his special brand of treatment. Ironically, despite being in such fine fettle, Brisbane was his one Test Match failure of the series. Boycott scored 37 and 16, falling to the spinners Gleeson and then Jenner, and compared to what followed it represented complete failure. Nevertheless, Boycott followed the drawn first Test with an innings of 126 against Western Australia. Then it was time for the second Test and on this latter occasion he proceeded to carry his marvellous form with him into the Test arena.

Perth was the venue and the game began with a partnership of 171 between Boycott and Luckhurst in four-and-a-half hours. Boycott batted in the opposite manner to the approach he had been using in the State games. He was rather subdued, allowing Luckhurst to dominate the stand and the Kent man went on to make 131 while Boycott, who was out first, made 70 including just three boundaries. However, Boycott's innings could not be deemed to be slow. On the contrary, it was Australia's Lawry who was in danger of getting batting banned on the grounds of inactivity! In the first Test he had batted for five-and-a-half hours while scoring 84 in the second innings and he played similarly at an equivalent stage of the second Test.

England reached 397 all out to which Australia had replied with 440 all out and, by virtue of an excellent 115* from Edrich, together with a sound 50 from Boycott, a declaration was possible that set Australia to score 245 runs for victory in two hours twenty-five minutes. It was not over-generous but Lawry was not even remotely interested. He scored 6 runs in sixty-eight minutes and only when Fletcher and Cowdrey bowled was the bat put to ball. Yet another Test Match had been reduced to boredom.

With the third Test well and truly drowned by rain the teams went to Sydney with no result to show; but Boycott and Snow were about to play the ace card for England. Luckhurst again opened with Boycott, with the same result as at Perth except that at Sydney the roles were reversed. Boycott overpowered the Australian bowling right from the start. Eleven boundaries were brilliantly stroked all around the wicket as Boycott made 77 out of the opening stand of 116 runs before he fell to a catch in the deep after hooking a long-hop from Connolly. Up to that point in the series it was the most totally controlled innings Boycott had played; some judges rated it the best he played in the entire series but, unfortunately from 201 for 2 wickets England slumped to 219 for 6 in little more than thirty minutes play with Ashley Mallett claiming 3 of the 4 wickets to fall, for 6 runs in 8 overs. Not for the first or last time it required the tail-end to rescue England. In due course the innings closed at 332 all out which was more than might have been expected after the earlier collapse.

England's mid-innings collapse however was as nothing when compared to Australia's first innings, for their last 6 wickets fell on the third morning for a paltry 47 runs. At 236 all out, the first innings gave England a substantial lead of 96 runs and Boycott was exactly the right person to whom Illingworth could turn. Batting precisely to orders (but after running out Edrich) his six-hours-and-fifty-minute vigil at the crease put England into an unassailable position. At one point the scoreboard read 48 for 3 wickets, but stands of 133 for the fourth wicket with D'Oliveira (56) and 95 for the fifth wicket with Illingworth (53) broke the Australian attack. Principally, the cause was Boycott. He wore the bowlers down, hitting a bare dozen boundaries in his series top-score of 142* but, most important of all, it enabled Illingworth to declare with 415 runs lead and more than nine hours playing time still left in which to bowl out Australia for a second time.

In the event, less than half of that time was required. Lawry (60*) was the sole Australian to withstand Snow, who, with startling accuracy, hit a worn patch on the wicket and made the ball kick viciously. His career-best Test performance of 7 for 40 included a spell of 5 for 20 in 8 overs on the last day as Australia crumpled and folded to 116 all out. This gave England victory by an overwhelming 299 runs. As the pitch was generally reckoned to favour spin more than pace it was an amazing performance by Snow and it stressed his accuracy as much as the pace and fire he possessed.

Disconcertingly, the series was marred at Melbourne by a combination of crowd trouble and, from an English point of view, such slipshod fielding that the tourists were fortunate to emerge with their 1–0 match lead intact. Although Australia amassed a first innings total of 493 for 9 declared, it was far more than they should have been allowed to achieve. Uncharacteristically, Colin Cowdrey at slip was the chief culprit. In the first innings alone he dropped four chances, including Ian Chappell twice when he was 0 and 14 and as he went on to make a century the errors were indeed costly. In all, England put down eight catches in the game with Cowdrey responsible for five of them. Far worse, however, was the crowd trouble which occurred at varying stages of the Test. When Chappell reached his century some 2,000 people stampeded on to the ground. In the resulting melée, Chappell's cap, Cowdrey's white hat and a stump were taken. Consequently, it was not too surprising when a good deal of disorder also erupted later in the game during England's second innings.

Long before that England had made 392 all out in reply to Australia,

1 **1974** *Test Trial at Worcester. Geoff Boycott (Yorks), John Lever (Essex) is the bowler.*

2 **1977** *Third Test, England v Australia, Trent Bridge. Geoff Boycott batting during stand with Alan Knott.*

3 **1977** *Fourth Test, England v Australia, Headingley. Geoff Boycott reaches his 100th first class century with this on drive off Greg Chappell.*

4 **1977** *Fourth Test, England v Australia, Headingley. Geoff Boycott scores his 100th first class century.*

5 **1978** *Second Test, England v New Zealand, Trent Bridge. Geoff Boycott.*

6 **1978** *Second Test, England v New Zealand, Trent Bridge. Geoff Boycott.*

7 **1978** *Second Test, England v New Zealand, Trent Bridge. Geoff Boycott acknowledges applause on reaching century.*

8 **1978** *Third Test, England v New Zealand, Lord's. Geoff Boycott.*

9 **1979** *First Test, England v India, Edgbaston. Boycott reaches century.*

10 **1978** *Geoff Boycott v Hampshire, Southampton.*

11 **1979** *First Test, England v India at Edgbaston. Boycott batting during his 155.*

12 **1980** *Geoff Boycott before the Test v the West Indies, The Oval.*

13 **1980** *Second Test, England v West Indies, Lord's. Geoff Boycott bowling, Lloyd backs up and Willey is the fielder.*

14　**1980** *Centenary Test, England v Australia, Lord's. Boycott cuts Pascoe.*

15   **1981** *Geoff Boycott batting v Barbados, Bridgetown.*

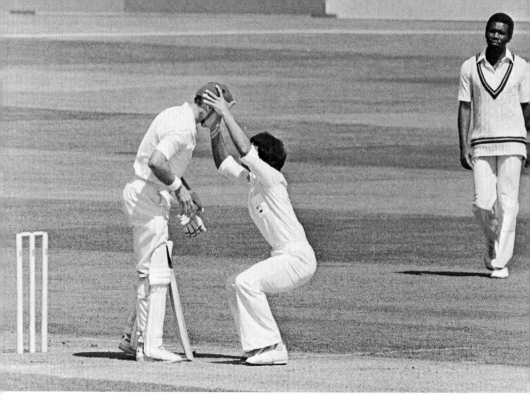

16 **1980** *Fourth Test, England v the West Indies, The Oval. Bacchus inspects Boycott after he had been hit by Croft. In spite of wearing a crash helmet, he suffered a cut about the eye.*

17 **1981** *Fifth Test, England v Australia, Old Trafford. Geoff Boycott with a hairy intruder.*

with Boycott recording a modest 12. The heroes of the hour were Luckhurst (109) and D'Oliveira, particularly Luckhurst who batted for the greater part of his five-and-a-half hour innings with a broken finger in his left hand. As D'Oliveira also later badly bruised his toe it meant that England were to be severely restricted in their second innings in the event of even a few wickets falling, but the ultra-defensive Lawry appeared not to want to win. His tactics of batting his team for four-and-a-half hours before declaring at 169 for 4 gave his bowlers little chance of bowling out England in the four hours of play that remained. Lawry could, with England reduced to nine fit batsmen, have set a much lower target than 271 and thereby given his bowlers a great deal more time to force the victory that could have squared the series. Instead, Boycott and Edrich had four hours in which to play as they chose. Unfortunately, the crowd did not like it.

Their attractive batting realised 161 runs without their being parted, with Boycott's 76* marginally shading Edrich's 74*. Off 45 overs they raced each other to a total of 133 but at that juncture the crowd began to demonstrate. The constant catcalls, jeering, slow handclapping and rattling of beer cans made concentration an impossible task therefore Boycott and Edrich responded by playing purely defensively. They could not be blamed for their actions. The behaviour of the crowd became so bad that the umpires discussed the situation but, perhaps wisely, they decided to allow play to continue.

What the crowd failed to realise, or did not want to, was that in conditions supposedly helpful to the spinners their slow bowlers had simply bowled badly. There was no other explanation and Boycott and Edrich duly profited even though there was little hope of their gaining a victory.

Thus to Adelaide, which proved to be Boycott's last Test of the series. Luckhurst was still injured, therefore Edrich was able to continue as Boycott's partner and in another drawn game they cemented their partnership with a century stand in each innings. The first amounted to 107 with Boycott making 58 when, ironies of ironies, he ran himself out! In the second innings he more than made up for the lapse by making a chanceless 119* with 103 runs coming between him and Edrich for the first wicket at a rate of nearly 5 runs an over. A measure of Boycott's own rate of scoring can be judged from the fact that his century was scored out of 169 runs. It contained eleven boundaries, took three-and-a-quarter hours to compile and came off 39 overs. In particular Boycott's hooking was very impressive in this innings. In certain respects it perhaps proved a point, for on more than one occasion in Tests he had been criticised for falling, too often it was said, to an injudicious use of that same stroke.

Surprisingly, Illingworth had not enforced the follow-on when he had been in a position to do so after the first innings thereby allowing

Boycott's second century of the series to stretch England's lead to an insurmountable 468 runs. There were eight hours and twenty minutes batting time left when Illingworth declared at 233 for 4, but the wicket, which was slow-paced, became progressively easier for batsmen. The wonder had been that England were able to bowl Australia out for 235 in their first innings, and the Aussies were certainly not going to capitulate as easily in the second. Redpath, with 21* in two hours, saw to that!

Their fourth draw out of five Tests marked the end of the tour for Boycott. The seventh Test was played, and won by 62 runs, without him and so was the New Zealand section. Injury again had taken its toll but not before Boycott had stamped his name indelibly into the minds of all the Australians who watched him, played against him and, perhaps most of all, bowled against him. It was the greatest series of his career.

Averages for 1970–71 Series v Australia

Tests	I	NO	Runs	HS	Avge
5	10	3	657	142*	93.85

Bowling: 1–0–7–0   **Centuries:** 2

Fielding: 4   **Half-Centuries:** 5

Cumulative Test Career Averages

Tests	I	NO	Runs	HS	Avge
46	80	12	3,266	246*	48.03

Bowling: 124–36–346–7   **Centuries:** 8

Fielding: 13   **Half-Centuries:** 18

Once home again Boycott, far from resting on his laurels, actually doubled his level of performance. It seemed like ever onwards and upwards. In the 1971 season Boycott scored *thirteen* centuries, more than double the number he had made on the other side of the world, and by September his total for the year, which was only a nine-month year at that, amounted to fifteen. More amazing still was Boycott's average for the season in all first-class matches – 100.12 which made him the first Englishman in cricket history to exceed the magical three-figure mark in all matches of English first-class season.

Very few counties were lucky enough to escape the wrath of Boycott's bat (or his tongue, in one instance) during that season, but Warwickshire and Middlesex suffered more than most, being hit for hundreds both at home and away. The first century against Middlesex, 112* at Leeds on 28 May, was the most noteworthy because it was the fiftieth first-class three-figure score of Boycott's career. However, the full catalogue of centuries is worth studying. From May to September 1971, Boycott's programme of centuries was as follows:

1. 110 for Yorkshire v Warwickshire at Middlesbrough in May

2. 112* for Yorkshire v Middlesex at Leeds in May
3. 169 for Yorkshire v Nottinghamshire at Leeds in June
4. 121* for England v Pakistan at Lord's in June
5. 233 for Yorkshire v Essex at Colchester in June
6. 182* for Yorkshire v Middlesex at Lord's in July
7. 112 for England v Pakistan at Leeds in July
8. 133 for Yorkshire v Derbyshire at Scarborough in July
9. 169 for Yorkshire v Lancashire at Sheffield in July
10. 151 for Yorkshire v Leicestershire at Bradford in August
11. 111 for Yorkshire v Hampshire at Bournemouth in August
12. 138* for Yorkshire v Warwickshire at Birmingham in September
13. 124* for Yorkshire v Northamptonshire at Harrogate in September

No less impressive were Boycott's full averages for 1971:

M	I	NO	Runs	HS	Avge	100's	50's	CT
21	30	5	2,503	233	101.12	13	6	6

In an otherwise high-class season there were two major low points for Boycott and in one instance the issue became both contentious and rather mystifying. First, of the six Tests played that summer by England against Pakistan and India, Boycott could play in only half of the games. He missed two Tests in the latter series because of a pulled hamstring, but also one match against Pakistan for a much more serious reason altogether. The episode, which turned into quite a trauma, began during the first Roses match of the season which was played at Old Trafford. The facts surrounding the affair, both at county level and later at Test level, were curious from whichever angle they are viewed.

Factually, the records show that Boycott did not bat in the second innings of the Roses fixture, ostensibly because he was ill. Doctors diagnosed nervous exhaustion when the condition came to light on the second day of the match. Significantly, that diagnosis followed hot on the heels of a stinging outburst Boycott had made criticising the Lancashire bowling tactics at Old Trafford. The net result was that Boycott did not bat on the last day which, for future reference was 1 June.

The Yorkshire Club issued their own statement to the effect that Boycott had been suffering from a heavy cold. The medical distance from nervous exhaustion to a heavy cold is quite large but an effort was being made to bridge the gap by the Yorkshire officials. All that happened, for whichever of the two illnesses was the prime reason, was that Boycott missed Yorkshire's next match, played at home on 2, 3 and 4 June against Worcestershire. However, he promptly returned to the side on 5 June against Nottinghamshire at Leeds and slammed 169 runs in the most vigorous manner possible. No matter how that week in the cricketing life of Geoffrey Boycott is viewed, there is room for scepticism. However, the orders for Boycott to rest did ring true because that period of inactivity a little later in June caused him to miss the first Test against Pakistan.

Not until Lord's in mid-June could Boycott return to the national side or continue onwards from the same Test point he had left behind him in Adelaide in February. Then he had scored 119*. Now, he matched it almost exactly, making 121*. Bad nerves, heavy colds or sheer bad-temperedness, they certainly did not appear to affect Boycott's Test Match temperament!

Due to the weather the Lord's Test against Pakistan was of little more than academic interest, notwithstanding Boycott contributing the ninth Test century of his career to the game. That it took him five hours ten minutes, spread over four days, is an indication of how much havoc was wreaked by the rain. Play could not start on the first day until mid-afternoon, there was less than half-an-hour possible on the second day and the third was washed out completely. As if that were not sufficient it was not until after lunch again on the fourth day that play could resume. In the periods of cricket that were played Boycott shared an opening partnership of 124 with Brian Luckhurst and did not give a single chance to the bowlers as he reached 121* before Illingworth called a halt to the innings at 241 for 2.

Even when Pakistan collapsed from 57 for 0 to 148 all out on the final day it was impossible to think in terms of an England victory. What time was left was fit only for batting practice but it was given over to Richard Hutton. He, instead of Boycott, opened the second innings with Luckhurst and the pair took the game to its logical conclusion with another century opening partnership, being worth 117 runs without either batsman being dismissed.

It was on Boycott's home territory, however, that a result became possible in the third Test at Leeds, although it went perilously close towards the end with the final difference between the sides amounting to only 25 runs in England's favour. If the result was good, so too was Boycott. Circumstances had conspired to give him a double victory; one for England and one himself. For on a personal level, Boycott had reached his peak. Moreover, it was his peak in terms of prolonged Test Match consistency. Headingley 1971 was indeed his summit, in as much as it marked also the end of a chapter.

In the first innings Boycott scored 112, hitting one six and fourteen fours. This was much more than just another Test Match hundred, or even the milestone of being his tenth in Tests. The figure ten held another significance but for very different reasons. Counting the 112 at Leeds, Boycott had, in his previous ten Test innings, accumulated 837 runs at an average of 139.50 per innings. Only once in those innings had he scored less than 50 and, of the four centuries three had come in successive visits to the crease. The first was against Australia (119*) followed by the two against Pakistan in England. Such figures underline that Boycott was a Test batsman of the very highest order. His deeds speak for themselves.

Averages for 1971 Series v Pakistan

Tests	I	NO	Runs	HS	Avge
2	3	1	246	121*	123.00

Bowling: **Centuries:** 2
Fielding: 0   **Half-Centuries:** 0

Cumulative Test Career Averages

Tests	I	NO	Runs	HS	Avge
48	83	13	3,512	246*	50.17

Bowling: 124–36–346–7   **Centuries:** 10
Fielding: 13   **Half-Centuries:** 18

That Boycott's scoring bubble had burst became patently obvious within two weeks of the Pakistan series ending. By that time the series against India had begun, but Boycott did not make a significant score in the first Test but that also proved to be his last Test appearance of the year. How swiftly the tide can change!

First, the Test Match. It was played at Lord's towards the end of July and although drawn it was a game always full of interest and not a little controversy. Boycott was not involved in this, but one of the main participants of an ugly mid-wicket confrontation was Sunil Gavaskar.

Gavaskar had recently burst onto the Test Match scene with four centuries and more than 700 runs in his first series in the West Indies. He was now making his first visit to England. This was Boycott's first meeting, therefore, with the man who was eventually to gain practically the whole range of Test batting records, including Boycott's own world Test record of runs scored in a career. However, more significant than runs at Lord's was the moment when Gavaskar, at the non-striker's end, was unceremoniously charged to the ground from behind by John Snow. Without much conviction Snow went to retrieve the ball on his follow-through after a sharp single had been called for and then seemed to switch his attention and his shoulder to Gavaskar. The England selectors summarily dropped Snow from the team for the second Test.

In this match India gained a first innings lead over England for only the second time in a Test Match in England. Boycott scored a negligible 3 before falling to a catch at the wicket off Abid Ali, and he fared little better the second time when, after reaching 33 Venkataraghavan tempted him into offering a catch to the Indian skipper Wadekar. The gift was not refused and with that dismissal, apart from holding a catch of his own in the Indian second innings, Boycott's Test Match summer was succinctly brought to a close. The Indians had required 183 runs to win but, with their score standing at 145 for 8 at tea on the last day, the game was left hanging in a tantalising balance by the return of the rain.

A week later Boycott was playing in a Sunday League match at Bradford for Yorkshire against Essex, just four days before the second Test was due to begin, when he pulled a hamstring whilst fielding. The injury immediately precluded him from playing in the Test and although he was actually selected for the third Test it was sufficiently nigglesome to keep him out of that game as well. Thus, his glorious run of runs had come to an end. Fittingly, perhaps, the run ended with Boycott's first Test Match encounter with Gavaskar. Boycott had shown what he could do, metaphorically, he had thrown down the gauntlet to Gavaskar and in the following ten years (inclusive of Boycott's three-year Test exile) Gavaskar would be the only batsman in world Test cricket worthy of the challenge. Sadly for Boycott, the superlative, diminutive Gavaskar would prove to be more than worthy.

Averages for 1971 Series v India

Tests	I	NO	Runs	HS	Avge
1	2	0	36	33	18.00

Bowling: **Centuries:** 0
Fielding: 1   **Half-Centuries:** 0

Cumulative Test Career Averages

Tests	I	NO	Runs	HS	Avge
49	85	13	3,548	246*	49.27

Bowling: 124–36–346–7   **Centuries:** 10
Fielding: 14   **Half-Centuries:** 18

7 Revenge at last on New Zealand

With England not touring during the winter of 1971–2 Boycott spent some of that time playing for Northern Transvaal in South Africa for whom, in February of 1972, he scored 107 against Rhodesia at Pretoria. In the early 1970s playing cricket in South Africa was not the hazardous occupation that it became a decade later. Nor could Boycott's playing for Northern Transvaal be mooted as the cause of the furore which erupted shortly before England toured India in 1981–2; for while the very fact that he, and others, had played in South Africa was the major cause of the wrangle it mattered little that Boycott played there in 1971–2. He had already toured the Republic in 1964–5 with an official Test party, therefore the storm would still have broken whether or not he played there again in later years. Furthermore, with having no obligations to either Yorkshire or England between the 1971 and 1972 home seasons Boycott was free to do as he pleased. Consequently, he was South Africa bound with the result that the sixty-second first-class century of his career was duly accomplished during an otherwise undistinguished season in the sun.

Six more centuries followed in England in the summer of 1972 but it was not altogether a happy time for Boycott. While he had a good season with the bat, 1,230 runs at 72.35 per innings, the runs were virtually all scored for Yorkshire, including each of the six centuries. Conspicuously absent were Test Match runs. In May, he hit 122* and 105 off Somerset and Lancashire respectively, then an exact 100 against Nottinghamshire in July, followed by 204* and 121 versus Leicestershire and Essex respectively. He rounded off the season with 105 at Southampton when Hampshire's attack provided the cannon fodder. However, the break in rhythm between May and July, or between the scoring of his second and third centuries of the season, was significant. In June Boycott played two Tests for England against Australia but immediately afterwards he suffered a serious hand injury. That put paid to any further Test appearances for the remainder of the summer.

The injury occurred not in a Test Match but whilst playing for Yorkshire in the first round of the Gillette Cup against Warwickshire at Headingley. The pitch that day was unusually lively and with Bob Willis

71

in full flight the ball was lifting quickly and dangerously. One such delivery from Willis rose viciously off the seam, and smashed onto Boycott's right hand. So great was the impact that a hole was ripped in Boycott's glove and the middle finger of the right hand was both crushed and cut.

For the last Test of the series Alec Bedser, Chairman of the England selectors, said that a place in the Test side was available to Boycott 'should he feel able to take it'. By that stage of the season, however, he had not played a first-class innings for five weeks and, although he scored a hundred in a Saturday League fixture shortly before the fifth Test, Boycott told Bedser that he would not be fit to play in the game. So Boycott had had scant opportunity to maintain his Test Match averages that season. In the first and second Tests he scored 8, 47, 11 and 6, no better than his two innings against India in the previous season. Indeed, Boycott's last six Test innings had failed to produce an aggregate as great as the last three-figure innings he had played in Test Cricket, in July 1971, when he made 112 against Pakistan. The two scores of 8 and 47 were made in Boycott's fiftieth Test appearance for England and, while something more substantial would have been a pleasant way to celebrate the milestone (à la Cowdrey, who scored a century in his hundredth Test for England) Boycott had to be content with an England victory instead. The tables were turned in the second Test with Australia squaring the series thanks mainly to the bowling of Massie and Lillee.

Obviously, no batsman can score a century or a fifty every time he walks to the crease, but Boycott's six-innings combination of low scores, in comparison to his immediately prior performances, did serve as the perfect example as to how swiftly the candle can be snuffed out in Test cricket.

Boycott would have to wait another year before getting back into the Test Match groove. However, if Boycott had to be out of Test cricket at all at that stage of his career, what better way for him to come back than to do so by laying the bogey of New Zealand once and for all.

Averages for 1972 Series v Australia

Tests	I	NO	Runs	HS	Avge
2	4	0	72	47	18.00

Bowling: **Centuries:** 0
Fielding: 0   **Half-Centuries:** 0

Cumulative Test Career Averages

Tests	I	NO	Runs	HS	Avge
51	89	13	3,620	246*	47.63

Bowling: 124–36–346–7   **Centuries:** 10
Fielding: 14   **Half-Centuries:** 18

In the twelve months that separated the second Test against Australia, in June 1972, and the first Test versus New Zealand, which commenced on 7 June 1973, Boycott missed not three but eleven possible appearances for England. In addition to the three 1972 Tests he had to forego because of injury Boycott opted out, on his own volition, of eight more internationals. These were played during the winter of 1972–3 when A. R. Lewis led an expedition to India, for five Tests, and Pakistan, where three Tests were played. By declining the tour Boycott was, whether by accident or design, giving a distinct impression that he was picking and choosing when, where and against whom he would play for England. It certainly did little to enhance his personal popularity amongst other England players, especially those who went to India and Pakistan, and one example from Lewis' tour showed their feelings in no uncertain terms.

On that tour some of the journeys between venues were made by coach, rather than by air, which entailed many hours of travelling. Boredom was alleviated to a certain degree, almost inevitably, by the players singing amongst themselves on the coach. One of the tunes readily employed was 'She'll be coming round the mountain when she comes . . .' However, with a slight alteration to the lyrics the words quickly became 'You can stick your Geoffrey Boycott up your . . .'! Some indication, perhaps, of what they thought of his refusal to tour India. For, in all probability, if any one of the players who did make the trip had turned down the invitation as Boycott had done they would not have been considered for England again. This was not to be so in Boycott's case, and for the new series against New Zealand, with a similar three-Test rubber against the West Indies to follow, Boycott was reinstated to his opening position for England. At Trent Bridge, in the first Test, another new batting partner went to the wicket with Boycott, Dennis Amiss, of Warwickshire. Amiss was the tenth different opening partner Boycott had had in his fifty-two Test career to date. They very nearly celebrated the new pairing with a three-figure stand but, after defying some extremely fine bowling from Bruce Taylor and Dayle Hadlee for the better part of three hours, the stand was broken at 92, when Boycott was trapped leg before wicket by Taylor for 51, which represented only the second half-century he had scored against the Kiwis in some thirteen Test innings. Perhaps the tide was turning at long last.

The New Zealanders, once they had made the initial breakthrough, performed with determined zest to dismiss England for 250 runs, but they immediately threw away their advantage by being bowled out for a meagre 97 runs. A huge fourth innings total for victory became the prospect facing New Zealand. A classic misunderstanding between Amiss and Boycott gave them, however, a great start in the England second innings. Amiss steadfastly refused to go for a second run while

Boycott, with equal resolution, continued to run until he was close enough to Amiss to hold a whispered conversation with him. The result:

G. BOYCOTT, RUN OUT 1.

Fortunately for England her batsmen rallied strongly to reach 325 for 8 before Ray Illingworth declared and set the New Zealanders 479 runs to win. Incredibly, they got to within 38 runs of this enormous task. From 130 for 4, Bev Congdon (176) and Vic Pollard (116) took the score to 307 for 5, following which Ken Wadsworth (46) stayed with Pollard until the score reached 402 for 6. Before Wadsworth was caught in the slips at that juncture the victory was within New Zealand's grasp but when Pollard also went, with the score at 414, England were able to scrape home to a shaky victory.

The issue at Lord's was again very close with New Zealand outplaying England. However, in this second Test of the series two typical Boycott innings and one of similar ilk from Fletcher saved the home team and they were able to hold on, precariously, for a draw. Fletcher's effort came in the second innings and it was an equally durable performance from Boycott in the first innings that saved the day after England had been put into bat in very humid conditions. Boycott batted with tremendous skill and application in conditions that would have had the vast majority of Test batsmen in difficulties. He scored 61 in a long stay at the wicket but it was the equivalent in value of a century under normal conditions. Unusually, there were two sixes amongst his boundary strokes, and he was going for a third when he lofted Collinge high to square-leg only for Parker to cling on to the catch. Without Boycott to hold the innings together England would have made much less than their eventual 253 all out. To judge from the manner in which New Zealand batted it was proven to be a crucial time-consuming innings.

New Zealand scored 551 for 9 declared, batting from early on the second morning until eighty minutes into the fourth day. Centuries from Congdon (175), Pollard (105*) and Burgess (105) made New Zealand's position impregnable and, facing a first innings deficit of 298 runs when they began batting a second time, England were involved in a desperate struggle to maintain their forty-four year unbeaten record against the Kiwis.

Boycott and Amiss went some way towards redressing the balance with their first century partnership adding 112 for the first wicket, until Amiss (53) gave a return catch to Hedley Howarth, the slow left-arm bowler. Boycott fell in a similar manner but not before he had progressed to 92 and the total to 185. The elusive century had been within two strokes of being his but he then hit a full toss straight back to Howarth. Fletcher then took the helm to score a brilliant 178 to steer England over a somewhat erratic course towards the draw: without the Essex man it would have been impossible. On the final afternoon England were no more than 70 ahead as the number ten batsman, Geoff Arnold, went out to join Fletcher. Although the latter fell, Arnold stayed until the close to see England through to 463 for 9.

Headingley staged the last Test of the series and Illingworth's men clinched the rubber by 2–0 with an emphatic innings victory, but the most heartening feature of the match from a Yorkshire point of view was Boycott's impeccable batting display, scoring 115 in England's one innings. At last a century against New Zealand! At last the Test 'Full House'! And it was accomplished with a touch of class, so much so, in fact, that many judges rated his 115 as one of Boycott's best centuries in his Test Match career. It was the eleventh Test hundred which, after fifty-four international appearances, meant that Boycott had scored at least one Test century against every Test playing country.

By his own standards the three-figure mark at Headingley was reached in a considerably faster time than usual. The innings lasted just three hours and twenty minutes. As the pitch had taken a four-hour downpour of rain on the second day, Boycott displayed a high sense of judgement, discretion and tempered aggression on such an obviously awkward wicket. Very few current players could have played better in the conditions.

In the three-Test series Boycott averaged 64.00 from five innings with his run-out at Trent Bridge being the only innings in which he failed to pass a half-century.

Averages for 1973 Series v New Zealand

Tests	I	NO	Runs	HS	Avge
3	5	0	320	115	64.00

Bowling: **Centuries:** 1
Fielding: 1   **Half-Centuries:** 3

Cumulative Test Career Averages

Tests	I	NO	Runs	HS	Avge
54	94	13	3,940	246*	48.64

Bowling: 124–36–346–7   **Centuries:** 11
Fielding: 15   **Half-Centuries:** 21

The second series of 1973 did not prove as bountiful for Boycott. He scored runs soundly enough on two occasions but that was all. By the end of the summer it had become obvious that the West Indies were a completely different calibre of opposition to New Zealand, but unfortunately that did not say a great deal for England. The Caribbean side was in a transitional period, still rebuilding a team from the remnants of their team in the 1960s. The series result, 2–0 in favour of the West Indies, was sufficient to illuminate England's deficiencies.

At the outset Boycott appeared to be continuing happily along the same groove as against the New Zealanders. In the first Test at the Oval he scored 97 in the first innings, which, while it could not prevent defeat by 158 runs, took him past a Test aggregate of 4,000 runs. The latest landmark had arrived in his 55th Test, thus enhancing how this middle period of Boycott's Test career was his most prolific in scoring terms. Boycott had taken thirty-two Tests to register his first 2,000 Test runs and only twenty-three Tests for the next 2,000 runs. In terms of innings the ratio was similarly different, the initial fifty-three having fallen to forty-two. One other quaint statistic emerged from the figures. In scoring 4,037 Test runs from ninety-five innings (inclusive of his 97 against the West Indies) Boycott had scored exactly twice as many half-centuries as he had centuries, with twenty-two fifties and eleven hundreds. Disappointingly, however, only controversy resulted from the last two Tests.

The second Test at Edgbaston was marred by an unseemly incident of which Boycott was the unwitting main cause and it foreshadowed other more disgraceful scenes in the third Test when he came very close to physical assault at the hands of the crowd. At Edgbaston, the centre of controversy was the umpire Arthur Fagg, who, on the second day, refused an appeal for a catch at the wicket against Boycott. The West Indies skipper Rohan Kanhai felt so indignant at this decision that he remonstrated publicly with Fagg for the two hours up to the close of play. For this open humiliation and hostility Mr Fagg felt he was owed at least an apology but it was not forthcoming. He threatened to withdraw from the match and went so far as to refuse to go out for the start of play on the third morning.

Diplomatic talks between Alec Bedser, Chairman of the England selectors, and Mr E. Kentish did eventually solve the problem but, in the meantime, Boycott's own worries had been further compounded by yet another painful injury. On the second evening, Boycott had collided with wicketkeeper Deryck Murray as he made a wild dash for the crease to beat a wild throw-in from Kallicharran. Although he was able to continue after a lengthy stoppage, soon after play started on the third morning Boycott had to retire hurt because of his bruised ribs. By that time he was 54* and enjoying a sound opening partnership with Amiss which had realised 105 runs. It was not until the ninth wicket fell at 302 that Boycott could continue his innings. Hence, an odd-looking England scorecard that suggested Boycott had batted through an innings of 300-plus for a personal score of only 56*! He added just 2 more runs to his own score before Underwood's wicket was claimed by Gibbs. The game resulted in a draw, and Boycott did not bat in the second innings.

The final Test at Lord's was a catastrophe for England. The game was lost in three-and-a-half days by an innings and 226 runs, the second heaviest margin of defeat in England's Test history. (Only at Brisbane in 1946–7 had England lost by a greater difference.) However, as the West Indies hit up 652 for 8 wickets in less than two days, even a draw was a forlorn hope at Lord's. Boycott's lack of success seemed to centre on his use of the hook shot which brought about his downfall in both innings. The first occasion saw him attempting the stroke to a ball rising outside the off stump with the result that he was caught in the slips by Kanhai for 4. Unfortunately, when a similar but better-struck shot caused the same effect in the second innings, off the last ball of the third day, Boycott received a dangerous amount of jostling from the crowd as he left the field. The shot may have been injudicious but it did not warrant such treatment of him by the hooligan element who were at Lord's that day.

In fact, when Boycott and Amiss began England's follow-on, 419 runs behind, with eighty-five minutes remaining on the third evening they batted with conspicuous ease for more than an hour. Suddenly, Keith Boyce summoned a supreme final effort of the day and, bowling from the pavilion end, dismissed Amiss, Knott and then Boycott at a cost of 6 runs in just 3.5 overs. The trap was set for Boycott by placing Kallicharran on the deep square-leg boundary, followed by the inevitable bouncer. Boycott took the bait, and hooked the ball straight into Kallicharran's hands. At that time of day, with England in a parlous status, it was a remarkably ill-conceived shot from a player of Boycott's skill, technique, experience, and normally cautious style.

Boycott still averaged 50 runs per innings against the West Indies, however. The one negative aspect was that he made 118 runs less from the same number of innings played against the West Indies than he had against New Zealand. Nonetheless, considering the results, it was not a bad series for him. What was perhaps much more ominous was the venue for the forthcoming winter tour of 1973–4. It was to the West Indies, but in typical dour Yorkshire style, Boycott would show that the Caribbean held few terrors for him.

Away from the Tests, Boycott's 1973 season had been the same mixture of ups and downs as the two Test series. There were five centuries in all, including 114 against the West Indies for D. H. Robins' XI at Eastbourne, but only two for Yorkshire in the County Championship. Cambridge University, 141*, the West Indies and New Zealand in the third Test were the 'outside' sufferers while Lancashire, 101, and Nottinghamshire, 129, glimpsed more of the true Boycott in the premier County tournament. However, as Boycott had shown throughout his career, it was an 'up and down' season only in relative terms. He finished the season with a healthy average of 63.62, with 1,527 runs in all first-class matches. There was still no other opening batsman in England to match him for his consistency.

Averages for 1973 Series v West Indies

Tests	I	NO	Runs	HS	Avge
3	5	1	202	97	50.50

Bowling: **Centuries:** 0
Fielding: 2   **Half-Centuries:** 2

Cumulative Test Career Averages

Tests	I	NO	Runs	HS	Avge
57	99	14	4,142	246*	48.73

Bowling: 124–36–346–7   **Centuries:** 11
Fielding: 17   **Half-Centuries:** 23

8 Towards the break

When Boycott's second tour of England duty in the West Indies began shortly after New Year 1974, few could have predicted the turmoil that lay in wait for him. He began as if he meant to surpass his earlier achievements in the Caribbean. In the very first first-class match he hit a career-best 261* against the Presidents' XI at Bridgetown (which still remains his highest first-class innings) but the hopes thereby raised were not quite fulfilled as the tour progressed, that is, if a final tour average of 73.85 can be classed as not reaching expectations!

Of the eleven first-class fixtures Boycott played in ten and his 960 runs from sixteen innings placed him second only to Amiss in the final averages. Included in those figures were 421 Test runs, at 46.77, plus three centuries, one of which was in the Test series. The third century, other than his 261* at Bridgetown and the fifth Test 112, came at Georgetown where Boycott scored 133 before retiring ill against Guyana. That century was his seventy-fifth in first-class cricket. The magical 'one hundred hundreds' was now on his horizon. But more immediate was the problem of the rubber against the West Indies following hard on the heels of a lost home series against the same opposition.

The first Test was lost by 7 wickets. England were put into bat at Port-of-Spain and the move brought instant reward for the West Indies with the early capture of Boycott's wicket. Yet again he fell to the hook shot. Boyce did the damage again after fifteen minutes of play and Boycott was caught by Julien for 6. England were in fact bowled out for 131 runs on that first day to confirm the wisdom of the West Indies' decision to invite the opposition to bat first. When the West Indies themselves made 392 all out, the last wicket falling early on the third morning, the game was almost beyond recall for England. Almost, because Boycott and Amiss viewed matters in a very different light. They batted throughout the remainder of the third day to raise their highest total of all their nineteen partnerships. As the stand was worth 209 runs it was only the second double-century opening Test partnership in which Boycott participated in his career.

Boycott was out within minutes of play resuming on the fourth morning, caught by Fredericks at short-leg, who took the catch off Gibbs' bowling. Gallingly, Boycott's 93 was the third occasion he had reached the nineties in Tests against the West Indies without actually managing to make the extra few runs to reach his hundred. Worse still, a fourth such score awaited Boycott in the fifth Test (also at Port-of-Spain) and to rub salt in the wound he would be 99 when dismissed. However, there was a happier sequel awaiting him in the same Test.

Following Boycott's dismissal in the first Test, England had reached 315 for 1 by lunch on the fourth day, holding thus a slender lead with 9 wickets intact, but by tea-time the advantage lay wholly with the West Indies as they sent England crashing to 378 for 8. While it was Sobers who began the slide by taking 3 wickets for 2 runs in fifteen deliveries, it was Gibbs who finally transformed the picture. After snaring Boycott and watching Sobers make the breakthrough, the off-spinner on analysis had 1 for 99. He finished the innings with 6 for 108!

All out for 392, England had only 132 runs to offer the opposition and although Underwood removed both Kallicharran and Lloyd in one over, Fredericks was in fine form. His 65* took West Indies to an easy victory and, apparently, to an easy rubber as well.

Prior to the second Test at Kingston there was a scare when Boycott had to retire hurt in the game against Jamaica. When 83* he was hit on the left arm by a bouncer from Dowe and that type of injury was becoming unusually common with Boycott. The same arm had once been broken by the Australian, Graham McKenzie. Possibly it was due to Boycott's technique. For the shorter-pitched deliveries his first movement has always been to move his right foot towards square-leg. Consequently, his body is not fully behind the ball. Usually, the method worked, but against the faster bowlers he would have a split second less to readjust his body and body-blows were difficult to avoid. However, it was to be a pulled muscle, not a broken arm, that was to hinder him most when the second Test got underway, also at Kingston.

In the first Test, Boyce had extracted sufficient life to 'bounce' Boycott. In the second Test, though, the pitch was very placid. England decided to bat first. Boycott made 68, which was also the extent of the opening partnership before Amiss was out. For much of his innings Boycott was hampered in his running by a pulled leg muscle. Of necessity, he had to take his time although it was in making a forceful drive off Sobers that he eventually lost his wicket. Kanhai was fielding at short mid-off and, with brilliant anticipation, he tumbled forward like an acrobat to take a marvellous catch. It was one of 5 wickets to fall on the first day. The remaining 5 followed on the next day and then the West Indies proceeded to bat until the fourth morning to establish a lead of 230 runs.

By the close on the fourth day England's position seemed to be hopeless. The score read 217 for 5 with only Amiss, Knott and the tail standing between the West Indies and another victory on the last day. Boycott had been out in the third over of the innings, caught behind the wicket for 5 off a Boyce bouncer as the ball grazed his glove when

Boycott took evasive action. With another four batsmen following him back to the pavilion before the day was over England appeared to have no hope left at all. Amiss, however, with the greatest Test innings of his career, showed that he too could 'do a Boycott' when required and his epic 262* saved a memorable match for England – with more than a little help from his friends at the bottom of the innings. First, the nightwatchman Underwood kept Amiss company for the first seventy-five minutes of the final day. Knott fell quickly when England were a mere 41 runs ahead but Chris Old remained at the crease for one hundred minutes to help Amiss add 72 runs for the eighth wicket. Finally, Pocock was virtually immobile for eighty-five minutes, for 4, and at the close England were 432 for 9. It was a cricketing version of 'The Great Escape' with Amiss playing the starring role.

The third Test at Bridgetown followed much the same pattern as the Kingston match. England again scraped a draw after being outplayed for most of the game and seeming to have lost but, that parallel apart, there was one very noticeable difference in this Test Match for Boycott, his 108th. This third Test of the 1973–4 tour was the *only* occasion in a Test Match when he played that Boycott did not open the innings. In both innings at Bridgetown he batted at number four in the order. There were two principal reasons. One was that it was a way to protect Boycott from the barrage of new-ball bumpers he continually received. Also, the move was an attempt to bolster the middle order, for England sadly lacked strength there.

On both counts the tactic failed. Julien and Sobers trapped Boycott with close to the wicket catches for 10 and 13 runs respectively, so that when the teams transferred to Georgetown for the fourth Test, following the second draw of the series, Boycott returned to his normal opening position. When thirteen hours of the fourth game were lost to rain, including all of the fourth day, the third successive draw meant that England were left with only the last game in which to square the series. Boycott, for his part, needed to pick up the pieces of a series that had not gone too well for him since the first Test. The drawn Georgetown game had afforded him only one innings in which Julien bowled him for 15, but there was some consolation that the fifth Test would be played at Port-of-Spain. On the 'horses for courses' theory Boycott could reasonably hope to do well there. His previous Test innings at the ground had produced scores of 68, 62, 80*, 6 and 93. It proved to be a thrilling match.

As the series was still undecided the fifth Test was extended to six days and Boycott himself went into the game quite out of form, but sheer determination saw him through to score 99 in six hours and twenty-five minutes in the first innings. He had one lucky escape. When on 9 he should have been run out by half the length of pitch by Kanhai, who had run from short-leg to fine-leg to field the ball, but his return was wild.

In a six-day match it was vital to England that at least one batsman should play a very long innings. Boycott, by batting purely defensively, was the ideal man for the occasion and, since no other batsman passed 50, Boycott's 99 out of an all out total of 267 had an immense bearing on the final result. However, on the third day the West Indies were cruising at 208 for 2 by lunch. Then Tony Greig transformed the match by taking 5 wickets in twenty deliveries. Lloyd, Sobers, Kanhai and Murray all went for the addition of 6 runs and, when Boycott intervened to catch Rowe (123) off a full-toss, again to Greig, the West Indies' stranglehold on the game had been cast off. In all, Greig captured 8 for 33 off 19.1 overs on the third day which was the reason the West Indies' lead on the first innings amounted to only 38.

Both Amiss and Denness were out with less than 50 on the board in England's second innings, the latter being dismissed at 44. Staunchly, Boycott and Fletcher (45) added 101 for the third wicket to alter once again the fluctuating fortunes both teams were experiencing. It was a most opportune moment for Boycott to place one more mark on to his growing list of Test records. That particular century partnership was his thirtieth such stand in Tests but at the fall of Fletcher's wicket two more batsmen came and went rapidly while only 7 runs were added to the total. Undaunted, Boycott seemed well-nigh invincible. When Boycott eventually did depart he had been at the crease for six-and-three-quarter hours and his monumental innings had yielded 112 precious runs. At last a Port-of-Spain century!

Unfortunately, there was rancour and controversy over Boycott's dismissal. In the records it is shown as 'bowled Gibbs 112' but, despite the leg bail lying on the ground, Boycott stayed at the crease for a long time after the event. Since the umpire, Sang Hue, had to consult with his colleague, S. Ishmael, at square-leg before giving Boycott out, there was obviously some doubt as to what exactly had taken place. Boycott played well forward to Gibbs' delivery. It later came to light that the ball had turned so sharply and so great a distance that Sang Hue's view of the stumps had been blocked by Boycott's outstretched pad. Therefore he checked with the square-leg umpire whether the ball had actually hit the wicket. Ishmael said yes, Sang Hue confirmed it with his finger and Boycott left having joined the select band of players who had scored a century and 99 in the same Test.

Such Test Match oddities produce interest. There are probably only a few worse disappointments to a cricketer than to miss by one run scoring two centuries in a Test Match. A 'pair', no doubt, or perhaps a century and 0 in the same game. But it is a great achievement for all that.

Boycott's part in the game was by no means finished however. Being 263 all out, England gave the West Indies a target of 226 runs to win and at the end of the fifth day they were 30 without loss, requiring 196 in the whole of the last day. A win was possible for either side, or a draw but a full day's play was unlikely. The game had already suffered many interruptions through rain but that had no great bearing on the last day. The question was, which side would better withstand the pressure.

Initially all went well for the home side, until Birkenshaw claimed the first wicket, that of Rowe leg-before, when 63 runs had been scored. Two deliveries later Kallicharran suffered the indignity of having a 'pair' inflicted upon him when he was caught at first slip off Greig. Then came the running out of Fredericks. The former Glamorgan player turned Birkenshaw past Boycott at square-leg. He ran one, turned for two and was allowed by Lloyd to advance ten yards down the wicket before Lloyd himself charged down the wicket. Fredericks, startled, hesitated and he was run out by yards after Boycott's throw. As a result, in 9 deliveries, 3 wickets had fallen for the addition of 2 runs. From that point the innings progressed to 84 for 4 and 85 for 5 wickets as Greig dismissed Lloyd and Kanhai. Although Sobers added 50 for the sixth wicket with Murray, the target had become too great. Inshan Ali (15) and Boyce (34*) took the score to 197 but once Lance Gibbs walked to the wicket, one of the world's veritable number elevens, it was only a matter of minutes before England had won an enthralling game to draw the series.

Two fine innings, coupled with his precision fielding, made Boycott's contribution a match-winning factor, and it went some way towards salvaging a disappointing tour. Yet it apparently failed to impress upon him the need to keep playing Test Match cricket. At the end of 1973, Ray Illingworth was replaced as captain by Mike Denness. Boycott only played one Test under Denness before taking leave of Test cricket.

Averages for 1973–74 Series v West Indies

Tests	I	NO	Runs	HS	Avge
5	9	0	421	112	46.77

Bowling: **Centuries:** 1
Fielding: 2   **Half-Centuries:** 3

Cumulative Test Career Averages

Tests	I	NO	Runs	HS	Avge
62	108	4	4,563	246*	48.54

Bowling: 124–36–346–7   **Centuries:** 12
Fielding: 19   **Half-Centuries:** 26

The Test which was to herald Boycott's departure from the highest level of the game was played in June 1974 against India. As Test Matches come and go, it was an average game. Centuries were made by Fletcher 123, Edrich 100*, and Gavaskar, 101; England won by 113 runs. Boycott took a very good running catch in India's second innings to dismiss Abid Ali, holding the ball as it dropped over his shoulder. That excepted, he was barely involved in the mainstream action. It was, however, no portent of the bombshell he was about to drop, nor did his two brief innings give any indication (small as they were) that they were to be his last Test innings for three years:–

G. BOYCOTT lbw   b. ABID ALI   10
     c. ENGINEER   b. SOLKAR   6

Nonetheless, just four days before the second Test against India, the newspaper headlines announced:

ENGLAND DROP BOYCOTT AND BRING IN LLOYD FOR SECOND TEST.

What the headlines did not say, however, was that this was no simple 'dropping' but a state of affairs which hid a much deeper meaning. For instance, John Woodcock, Cricket Correspondent of *The Times*, wrote illuminatingly, if not entirely correctly, at the time: 'The England selectors have given Geoffrey Boycott a rest from Test cricket by leaving him out of the side to play India at Lord's next Thursday . . . I am sure it is out of kindness to Boycott that he has been given a break . . . But if I had money on Boycott getting a Test hundred before the summer is out I would have few qualms yet.'

Three weeks later the picture had changed considerably, and John was now writing: 'There is still no Geoffrey Boycott in the England side announced yesterday for the third and final Test match against India, beginning at Edgbaston next Thursday . . . When his story comes to be told – and goodness knows what turns it has still to take – his changing fortunes as an England cricketer in the last year alone will fill a chapter . . . When Boycott was left out after the first Test against India earlier this month, *following a long conversation with Alec Bedser . . .*'

The last phrase was of paramount importance, for it was tacit confirmation that Boycott himself did not want to play for England. There are several points to consider. The first report indicates that Boycott had not opted out of the England team, merely that he had been 'rested'. (Why this should be is beyond comprehension, for Boycott had just scored a century in each innings of the recently resurrected Test trial at Worcester, batting for an England XI v The Rest). The second point – Mr Woodcock's absence of qualms on a Boycott century would have cost him dearly – followed on from and seemed to confirm the first point. More seriously, however, in the space of a few weeks it had become clear that Boycott failed to regain his place because he was originally omitted at his own suggestion after a discussion with the Chairman of the England selectors.

Whatever the reasons *out* means *out* and out was where Boycott stayed from 11 June 1974 until 28 July 1977, during which period England played thirty Test Matches at home and abroad.

Two of the main reasons advanced by the press for this self-imposed exile were Boycott's failure to gain the captaincy of England when it became vacant in 1973 (which was always his cherished ambition) and his inability to play under Mike Denness. Either theory could have been correct, or it could have been a combination of both, or both could have been way off the mark. Certainly, when Illingworth stepped aside in 1973, Boycott, as the current Yorkshire skipper, would have had his supporters for the England captaincy. As Denness was given the job, Boycott's leadership qualities were presumably not considered to be strong enough. Whether or not Boycott could get along with Mike Denness was quite another matter.

There were press reports which said that Boycott had no respect for Denness either as a man or as a cricketer, and there was always a bevy of reporters willing to make great issue of the point that Denness was not English, but Scottish. It was not too surprising that Boycott could not 'communicate' with an England skipper. There were times enough during his career when he did not seem too friendly with his own shadow. There were, no doubt, several other inter-related reasons but they can be revealed only when the man himself decides to speak openly. That will probably only occur when he writes and publishes his own book. Until then, it seems better to concentrate on the cricket which Boycott played rather than on questions which cannot be answered finally.

Therefore, it has to suffice for the present to say that Boycott went into the Test Match wilderness. Sadly, the undivided attention he now gave to Yorkshire cricket seemed to be of little benefit to the club – the former champions still won nothing, as had been the case since 1969. Conversely, Boycott himself prospered. He finished the 1974 season with an average of 59.43 (1,783 runs and six centuries), 1975 with an average of 73.65 (1,915 runs and another six centuries), and 1976 with an average of 67.78 (1,288 runs and five centuries), so that by 1977 he had ninety-three first-class centuries to his name.

That golden hundredth hundred was now within reach; and all the signs were that he intended, if possible, to reach it in the manner most suitable to him – that is, in a Test Match.

Averages for 1974 Series v India

Tests	I	NO	Runs	HS	Avge
1	2	0	16	10	8.00

Bowling: **Centuries:** 0
Fielding: 1   **Half-Centuries:** 0

Cumulative Test Career Averages

Tests	I	NO	Runs	HS	Avge
63	110	14	4,579	246*	47.69

Bowling: 124–36–346–7   **Centuries:** 12
Fielding: 20   **Half-Centuries:** 26

9 The greatest moment

While 1976 had mostly been one long, uninterrupted spell of sunshine, the opposite proved to be the prevailing weather for the 1977 cricket season. For Boycott's fans the summer promised to be full of interest. There was speculation that he might return to the England side now that Michael Brearley had been appointed captain. Also, there was the prospect of his scoring the seven centuries he needed to reach one hundred hundreds in first-class cricket. That would be difficult enough to perform in any single season under good conditions but given the atrocious weather experienced in April, May and early June the mission appeared to be virtually impossible to complete by September.

Not until 20 June did Boycott register his first century of the season. It was Boycott's ninth match and only his tenth innings of the summer. In the county match versus Derbyshire Boycott did not bat at all, whilst against Northamptonshire and Lancashire he was dismissed without scoring in his sole visit to the crease. Consequently, when Yorkshire met Somerset at Harrogate, commencing on 18 June, Boycott had had precious little batting all season. Only three scores (including 70 and 74 in the away fixture with Northamptonshire) had been above 50. In the circumstances Boycott had performed quite well to aggregate 314 runs at an average of 44.85 per innings.

At Harrogate the situation was remedied perfectly in an exciting 4-wicket win by Yorkshire over Somerset which was achieved in hectic style in a second innings run-dash. Boycott's long awaited opening hundred of 1977 had materialised earlier in the game in Yorkshire's first innings when he made 139*, which included a third wicket stand of 176 with Jim Love (89). He followed it with 60 at the second time of asking when quick runs were required. Thus, with victory adding a welcome bonus, his ninety-fourth century was accomplished.

A fortnight later Yorkshire met the touring Australians at Scarborough. Boycott invited the Aussies to bat and the faith he showed in his bowlers was rewarded as the visitors were hustled out for 186 runs. Unfortunately, that total was made to look relatively huge when Yorkshire fared terribly against Max Walker (5 for 29) and Mick Malone (4 for 38) who dismissed Yorkshire for a disastrous 75 all out, with Boycott failing to score. Everything went much better for both teams, however, the second time around. Australia made 215 for 7 declared to offer Yorkshire

327 to win at 65 runs per hour. Although Yorkshire never took up the challenge Boycott dominated their second innings for four-and-a-half hours. In that time he advanced to 103, with the aid of sixteen boundaries, before falling leg-before to Bright, and achieved a fair draw.

From Scarborough, Yorkshire travelled to Lord's to play Middlesex. By this stage of the season Boycott was settling firmly into a groove. After Middlesex used nearly all of the first day compiling 256 all out, Boycott was fortunate to be dropped behind the stumps off Daniel, when 4. On the second day, he went on to make 117, but, it took him 96 overs to achieve a laborious century, and he appeared completely to disregard the option of gaining batting bonus points by scoring faster. He gave more ammunition for the growing band of critics who despaired at Boycott's self-edifying but negative tactics, and who objected to his scoring rate of only one run per over. Nevertheless, if nothing else, the innings had duly obtained his ninety-sixth century.

The most frustrating aspect of this situation was that Boycott, in the very next match, took Yorkshire to a marvellously thrilling victory. This game took place at Trent Bridge, where the home side gained a first innings lead of 79 runs. P. D. Johnson (106*) and M. J. Smedley (130*) then further enhanced their side's position with a dramatic unbroken second-wicket partnership of 243 runs which enabled Smedley to declare at 243 for 1 and set Yorkshire the seemingly impossible target of 323 runs to win in four hours and forty minutes. In complete contrast to the dismal display at Lord's, Boycott went all out for the runs and his side got home with ten minutes and 5 wickets to spare.

This fine performance showed that, when he wanted to, Boycott could do it. With Barrie Leadbeater (71), 176 runs were rapidly accrued for the first wicket. Sidebottom also chipped in with 57* but it was Boycott's sterling innings of 154 which was the foundation of Yorkshire's success. There, in glorious style, was his ninety-seventh century.

In the meantime, England was busily engaged in beating Australia by 9 wickets at Old Trafford. It was the second Test of the series. The first, or Jubilee Test celebrating the Silver Jubilee of Her Majesty Queen Elizabeth II, had been drawn at Lord's. The victory at Manchester followed and then came the announcement of the year – Boycott would play cricket again for England. He had finally decided the time was ripe for him to return.

The comeback of the veteran was marked at the opposite end of experience by the Test debut of a young man named Ian Terence Botham who, within a very short space of time, was into his stride: indeed, almost from the moment Australia began the match by batting first. From a relatively safe position of 131 for 2 Australia slumped, principally due to Botham, to 243 all out. He took 5 for 74, including a spell of 4 for 13 in thirty-four deliveries, and England were well on their way to another victory. Boycott, however, did not allow young Botham to steal all the thunder.

Australia's rapid dismissal brought Boycott to the crease before the close of play on the first day. He went on to bat on all five days of the Test. He spend more than twelve hours at the wicket, and only M. L. Jaisimha of India had previously achieved the feat, when playing also against Australia at Calcutta in 1959–60. Boycott's efforts produced 187 runs for only one dismissal. There was no denying that he was permanently back in the Test arena.

Yet, it was not all plain sailing for him. England had begun their reply to Australia by stuttering to 82 for 5. In succession Boycott lost Brearley (15) at 34, Woolmer (0) at the same score, Randall (13) at 52, Greig (11) at 65 and Miller (13) at 82. Randall's dismissal, however, incurred the tempestuous wrath of the Nottinghamshire crowd. What happened could only occur with a player such as Boycott who seemed continuously to court controversy, for, incredibly, he *ran out* Derek Randall. Boycott called for a suicidal run (he admitted afterwards that it was entirely his fault), he charged down the wicket, Randall paid the penalty and the crowd bayed its anger like a pack of bloodhounds scenting a kill.

From 1964 to 1973 Boycott had built up a horrendous reputation for his running of sharp, ill-chosen singles. The batsmen who had fallen foul of his folly were innumerable although Bob Barber (see Chapter 3), prior to Randall, would probably award first prize to his own run-out. In this his very first match back in the England team Boycott did it again. Furthermore, whilst any run-out would have been bad enough, for it to be Randall, on his own ground, meant that the error was compounded. Therefore, as Randall walked dejectedly away, Boycott stood, head in hands in stunned disbelief. His only means of atonement would be to go on and make a century.

When Miller was replaced by Alan Knott, Boycott had batted resolutely for three hours. It was obvious he was going to dig in after the Randall disaster but he needed someone to stay with him if it was to be of any use to England. Knott was ideal for this. Already Boycott had ridden his luck, for almost immediately after being joined by Knott he was dropped in the slips by McCosker off Pascoe. If one dropped catch can turn a Test Match, it was that fielding error around which the Trent Bridge Test revolved. By close of play (which came thirty minutes early because of bad light) Knott and Boycott had added 160 priceless runs in three hours less five minutes, and England had regained the initiative. It was fairy-tale Test cricket, the province of comic-strip writers, but on this occasion the air of reality about the proceedings was all too real for the Australians.

The next day Knott began at 87 and went on to make his hundred. Boycott, began at 88 and reached his century soon afterwards. Their stand eventually realised 215 runs to equal the previous highest England–

Australia sixth-wicket record established by Hutton and Hardstaff at The Oval in 1938, but no sooner was the record equalled than Boycott fell to a slip catch off Thomson. Ironically the catcher was McCosker. Boycott had made 107 and it signified a brilliant return to Test cricket. Not to be out-done, Knott continued on his way to register, with 135, the highest individual score by an England wicketkeeper against Australia, and by mid-afternoon England had reached 364 all out, a lead of 121 runs.

Australia batted undemonstrably for the remainder of the day to close at 112 for 2 with McCosker batting particularly soundly. He continued long into day four to compile an exactly similar score to the Boycott he had dropped, in a very similar time too (with one six and ten fours) but while several other batsmen stayed with McCosker for lengthy periods, none succeeded in passing 50. Consequently, Australia were bowled out for 307 to give England a full day plus a little more in which to make 189 runs to go 2–0 up in the series. With no fuss Boycott and Brearley scored 17 runs before stumps were drawn.

There appeared to be few problems for England to overcome on the fifth day apart from the weather (thundery showers was the forecast) and much negative bowling from the Australians. Despite these tactics, for a while there was the tantalising prospect of victory by the unexpected margin of 10 wickets as Brearley and Boycott steadily took their opening partnership past the 150 mark. It was only when trying to force the pace, at 154, that Brearley fell to Walker for 80 when he played the ball on to his stumps. Walker took 2 more wickets, Greig (0) and Knott (2), to claim three scalps in the space of six deliveries. It was all to no avail however, Randall this time survived with Boycott.

It was cricket's form of poetic justice that the victim and the villain of the piece from the first innings should be together when England won. With Boycott quite passive, Randall guided his side home, made the winning hit, and then strode off the field arm-in-arm with his erstwhile Danger Man! With 80* in the second innings, Boycott had, at one stage, the possibility of recording his second century of the match; but he had now scored ninety-eight first-class centuries, of which thirteen had been made in Test Matches.

Fresh from his Test triumph Boycott continued in good form for Yorkshire. When, in his last match for the county before the third Test began at Headingley, another Test centre, Edgbaston, provided the stage for another hundred, when, on the second day of a rain ruined game, Boycott scored 104, in company with Jim Love who made 129, during Yorkshire's first innings. This encounter with Warwickshire became renowned for the remarkable second innings of Chris Old when the home side were attempting to induce a finish to the game. Old was fed a diet of full tosses by Warwickshire's batsmen suddenly turned bowlers. Old was able to hit six sixes and thirteen fours as he raced to his hundred in thirty-seven minutes, the second fastest century in the history of first-class cricket. The second 50 runs were scored by Old in an amazing *nine* minutes but, for all of his exertions, Boycott declined Alvin Kallicharran's offer of a possible victory and the game was drawn.

So now a unique opportunity awaited Boycott. He could hope to become the first man in Test history to score his one hundredth first-class hundred in a Test Match. For good measure, the opportunity arose on his own home ground. Public interest was immense.

To judge by the crowd which thronged Headingley and the atmosphere they generated at the start of the fourth Test there was hardly anybody present who did not feel they were about to witness a unique piece of cricketing history. When Brearley won the toss and elected to bat the air of expectancy and hope was intense. The crowd sensed that Boycott was destined to go to the wicket and score a century and the fans would not or could not countenance otherwise.

The crowd's sense of inevitability showed itself to be entirely justified. Throughout the innings partners came and went but Boycott stayed, seemingly, forever. Brearley lasted no more than three deliveries, dismissed by a catch to Marsh off Thomson. On the other side of the coin Boycott was intractable. By lunch he had made 34. At tea he had scored one more run in the session to reach 69. Then, after five hours and twenty minutes at the crease and from the 232nd delivery he faced, Boycott on-drove Greg Chappell, nearly straight, to the boundary. Headingley went wild. Boycott had finally carved his own niche into the history books. Other records would be broken but this would remain with him for evermore.

'Where were you when Boycott scored his hundredth ton?' became a famous question in Yorkshire. If the person concerned was not actually at Headingley to see the event then the chances are that most Yorkshire-men (and a goodly number of Yorkshirewomen too) will still know exactly where they were or what they were doing at precisely 5.49pm on Thursday 11 August, 1977. For that was the moment when Boycott officially achieved his claim to cricketing greatness.

When play ended on the first day England had reached 252 for 4 with Boycott 110* and Graham Roope 19*. The second day progressed in much the same fashion as England relentlessly pursued their way to 436 all out. Apart from Boycott, the highlight of the day was another sixth wicket partnership between him and Alan Knott. On this occasion they added 123 runs before Knott fell; but Boycott, remained right to the end of the innings to be the last man out. He batted for almost ten-and-a-half hours, hit twenty-three boundaries and his 191 runs was the second highest score of his Test career.

Scoreboard: England v Australia
Played at Headingley, Leeds, August 11, 12, 13, & 15, 1977

England 1st Innings

J. M. Brearley	c. Marsh	b. Thomson	0
G. Boycott	c. Chappell (G. S.)	b. Pascoe	191
R. A. Woolmer	c. Chappell (G. S.)	b. Thomson	37
D. W. Randall	LBW	b. Pascoe	20
A. W. Greig		b. Thomson	43
G. R. J. Roope	c. Walters	b. Thomson	34
A. P. E. Knott	LBW	b. Bright	57
I. T. Botham		b. Bright	0
D. L. Underwood	c. Bright	b. Pascoe	6
M. Hendrick	c. Robinson	b. Pascoe	4
R. G. D. Willis		Not Out	5
		Extras B 3 LB 9 NB 22	39
		TOTAL	436

Fall of Wickets

1	2	3	4	5	6	7	8	9	10
0	82	105	201	275	398	398	412	422	436

Bowling	O	M	R	W
Thomson	34	7	113	4
Walker	48	21	97	0
Pascoe	34.4	10	91	4
Walters	3	1	5	0
Bright	26	9	66	2
Chappell (G. S.)	10	2	25	0

England won by an innings and 85 runs.

When the second day was over the match was as good as completed. Australia had fallen away to 67 for 5 and the issue was quickly resolved to 103 all out early on the Saturday morning. For Australia to follow-on was the sole logical conclusion. Brearley's optimism was well founded, because two of the second innings wickets fell before the luncheon interval and Greg Chappell alone was able to demonstrate how to play the swinging ball. For a great deal of the time the light was very poor. As a result, nearly all of the last session of play was lost to the weather, which did not improve to any marked degree over the weekend and it gave Australia some hope, even if false, of salvaging a draw.

Play was not resumed on the fourth day until 2.00pm, with Australia at 120 for 4. Immediately their hopes of survival nose-dived. Chappell was dismissed for 36, after giving his team a perfect exhibition of how the conditions could be countered. Marsh hit lustily for 63 (he had little alternative) but it was no more than a typical gesture of defiance. His stand of 65 for the eighth wicket with Walker raised the total to a respectable 248 although it was still some 85 runs short of making England bat again. Marsh was last out when he skied a ball from Hendrick wide of mid-off and the irrepressible Randall judged a difficult running catch to perfection. Randall promptly performed a celebratory cartwheel, not only to emphasise the innings victory but also the fact that England had regained the Ashes.

The final drawn fifth Test proved to be an anti-climax to all that had gone before. Boycott scored 39 and 25* respectively in each innings to boost his aggregate for three Tests out of the five in the full series to 442 runs. His batting average of 147.33 per innings was far and away the highest he was to achieve from any series in his career. His comeback had been magnificent. Taking into consideration the previous fourteen years, and his great individual innings as well as his powerfully sustained efforts over a complete series, 1977 can be judged as the pinnacle for Boycott. He worked to his own pace, came back when he wanted to, and rode the pressure with an aplomb and professionalism that has to be admired, for its sheer tenacity if not for any feeling of human warmth. It was the culmination of what he had striven for so relentlessly since he first played for Yorkshire in 1962.

Next on his agenda had to be Garfield Sobers' world Test aggregate record, for there was no other target upon which to set his sights.

Averages for 1977 Series v Australia

Tests	I	NO	Runs	HS	Avge
3	5	2	442	191	147.33

Bowling: **Centuries:** 2
Fielding: 0   **Half-Centuries:** 1

Cumulative Test Career Averages

Tests	I	NO	Runs	HS	Avge
66	115	16	5,021	246*	50.71

Bowling: 124–36–346–7   **Centuries:** 14
Fielding: 20   **Half-Centuries:** 27

10 A sudden change of heart

As Boycott was now back in the England team he would presumably want to keep that place for as long as possible. Also, hand in hand with continued selection went Boycott's intention to challenge Garfield Sobers' run Test aggregate record of 8,032 runs. Boycott was now rising thirty-seven and although he still had a long way to go (some 3,000 Test runs), with his fitness and ability there was no reason why he should not pass that record; but only if he accepted such tours, which he had refused in the past, as those to Pakistan and India. Which, of course, is precisely what he chose to do.

The 1977–8 tour was a double-barrelled affair with three Tests being played in both Pakistan and New Zealand. Of a total of fifteen first-class games Boycott played in all but two and in four of the Tests achieved every cricketer's ambition of leading the national side. It was no more than a mixed blessing, however. The distinction would go down in the annals of cricket history for the wrong reasons.

Boycott began the tour in prime form. He went into the first Test with two successive centuries behind him having scored 123* against a United Bank XI and 115 versus the North-West Frontier Governors XI.

The most entertaining aspects of the first Test at Lahore were, unfortunately, the riots which interrupted play on two separate occasions. The first innings was not completed until fifteen minutes before lunch on the fourth day, during which time Mudassar Nazar spent nine hours and seventeen minutes compiling the longest century in the history of Test cricket. And the record may not have stood for much longer than the innings itself for Boycott took four hours and fifty minutes to reach 50 and only a brilliant delivery from Iqbal Qasim on the shirt-front pitch (the ball turned from the line of the middle stump to hit the off) prevented Boycott from crawling past Mudassar's newly established record.

On the riot scene, the main interruption occurred on the second afternoon when, with Mudassar on 99, the crowd invaded the pitch for a premature celebration of his century. The police intervention was summarily swift and brutal and running fights broke out in all parts of the field, but the crowd must have gained the upper hand. Four of the same police who had been eager to use their lathi sticks took refuge in the England dressing room! Then there was an amazing about-turn. The rioters voluntarily cleared the ground of debris to enable play to be resumed and less than half-an-hour of actual play was lost. But it made little effective difference. The end-result was always going to be 'boredom drawdom'. Batting such as that of Mudassar and Boycott advertised that all of the Tests would be similarly drawn.

At Hyderabad there was a slim possibility of a result until Pakistan's captain Wasim Bari took his country's motto of 'we shall not lose at home' to the extreme. Despite two exhilarating innings from Haroon Rashid (108) and Javed Miandad (88*) to force home the advantage, Wasim Bari did not declare until twenty minutes from the close of play on the fourth day.

After Pakistan made 275 all out England were bewildered by the wily Abdul Qadir, who exploited the footmarks left by Willis, and they were bowled out 84 runs short of their first innings target. Boycott made 79 before running himself out while Qadir took 6 for 44. England's aim was for a draw; they were never going to make any attempt to score 334 in 330 minutes or anything else approaching that rate.

In the event Boycott and Brearley had few worries. Of the two century first-wicket partnerships they shared together while opening for England, their 185 at Hyderabad was much the higher. Brearley was out for 74 while Boycott went on to register the century he had already twice threatened to score in the series, but it was only made possible by a delightful sporting touch that was added to the proceedings. Towards the end of the last day, although there was no result possible, the teams stayed on the pitch to allow Boycott to complete his century. The Pakistanis could have called it a day when the time arrived for the mandatory last fifteen overs to be bowled. Instead, Boycott was given his chance and when, off the third ball of the twelfth over, his goal was reached the game immediately ended. It was his third (and last) Test hundred against Pakistan. It was also his third in Tests from the five matches and eight innings since his comeback.

At this juncture of the tour fate intervened to hand Boycott the England captaincy although he was very quick to point out in an interview that while he was pleased to realise an ambition, he was well aware that it was due to the most unfortunate of circumstances. Mike Brearley was playing in a one day work-out game against Sind XI at Karachi three days before the final Test when he broke his left arm. He was hit by the one ball that rose any height at all in the full day's play, off Sikander Bakht. Brearley returned to England that same evening. Boycott took over command straight away but the drama did not end there. His first Test as England captain might never have seen a ball bowled at all, for three of Pakistan's 'Kerry Packer' players were seen at the nets immediately prior to the game. The England party objected in the strongest possible terms. Feelings were running high then on the

Packer issue and if the three players concerned (Mushtaq Mohammad, Zaheer Abbas and Imran Khan) had not been withdrawn from selection the Test would probably have been cancelled.

As if that were not enough, when the game was finally played and left drawn, Boycott took his first Test as leader as an opportunity to launch a scathing attack on the host country's arrangements. The Karachi wicket, the continual distractions and interruptions during the game and, most undiplomatic of all, Pakistan's apparent belief that defeat would constitute a national disaster were all criticised.

What took place during the game was that England batted for nine-and-a-half hours in scoring 266 all out, with Boycott being bowled by Iqbal Qasim for 31. When Pakistan batted they took a marginal lead of 15 runs but so much time had elapsed for the first innings to be completed that the game was well into its fourth day. The last day became a farce. Play began late, only 8 overs were bowled in the first hour. It was obvious that the match would never have a result, as Boycott ably demonstrated by going through a spell of 18.7 overs with only one scoring stroke. By mutual agreement play ended one hour early.

While there had never been the remotest possibility of a result in Pakistan, it was to be quite the opposite situation in New Zealand. The Pakistan series produced little more than sets of statistics. The crowd provided more excitement than the players. It all seemed rather pointless. In retrospect, despite the inconclusiveness, Boycott would probably have preferred three more Tests of the same type, rather than play the first Test in New Zealand. In that match, after forty-eight years of England–New Zealand Tests, England lost for the first time. Boycott was the unfortunate captain and the result gave his growing army of critics even more ammunition.

Averages for 1977–78 Series v Pakistan

Tests	I	NO	Runs	HS	Avge
3	5	1	329	100*	82.25

Bowling: 3–0–4–0   **Centuries:** 1
Fielding: 0   **Half-Centuries:** 3

Cumulative Test Career Averages

Tests	I	NO	Runs	HS	Avge
69	120	17	5,350	246*	51.94

Bowling: 127–36–350–7   **Centuries:** 15
Fielding: 20   **Half-Centuries:** 30

Having played in the opening fixture against Auckland, Boycott missed the next match versus Central Districts. After making 7 off the Canterbury attack, however, he was hit twice on his left arm and compelled to retire hurt. He resumed his innings at the fall of the seventh wicket and was eventually last out for 11. Once more, it seemed, Boycott was having a less than happy time in New Zealand.

The first Test at Wellington was eventful from the very start, and in the later stages wickets tumbled in stunning fashion. New Zealand batted first to make 228, but England were unable to overhaul this modest total despite Boycott making his highest Test score, from five appearances, in New Zealand. His innings lasted for seven hours and forty-two minutes, during which time, when he reached 61, Boycott passed Sir Jack Hobbs' aggregate of 5,410 Test runs. Seven runs after that Boycott was hit above the eye whilst attempting to hook Richard Hadlee. Under the circumstances it was a decidedly risky shot for him to play, for, throughout the greater part of his innings, Boycott had been forced to endure the pain and irritation caused by grit behind his contact lenses. It must have made batting extremely awkward, hence his hourly scoring rate of 10, 12, 6 and 12 again in each of four of the seven hours he spent at the crease. However, as the England innings drifted to 215 all out the value of his 77 runs could not be offset against the time it took him to compile them.

The rapid fall of the last 4 English wickets was a prelude to more dramatic events which were to follow. New Zealand collapsed in their second innings from 82 for 1 to 123 all out. However, this was as nothing compared to England's performance. Requiring 137 runs for victory the side could muster barely half of that total and the rot set in even as early as the twelfth delivery of the innings. Boycott then attempted to drive Collinge, but misjudged the line of the ball and was bowled off his pads. From that point New Zealand gained heart by the minute while England fell into complete disarray.

The innings had begun at tea on the fourth day and by the close England had scored 53 for 8 wickets which, in effect, was for 9 wickets because Rose had retired hurt. Although a frustrating forty minutes had to be spent in the dressing-room on the last morning, due to the weather, New Zealand duly accomplished the most extraordinary win in their Test history.

The result may have been a calamity for English cricket. England bowled out for 64 pathetic runs when needing only 137 runs to win in four sessions of play! But it was a calamity too for Boycott. If he had held any lingering aspirations of taking over the England captaincy permanently (which seemed unlikely to happen) that result at Wellington had destroyed any such hopes. Not even a victory at Christchurch in the second Test, by 174 runs, could erase the catastrophe of Wellington.

Christchurch belonged to Ian Botham. He scored his maiden Test century, took 8 wickets for 111 runs in the match and held three second-innings catches. It was a great all-round performance. Boycott made 8 and 26 in his only victory when leading England; and while another half-century lay around the corner for him in the drawn third Test at

Auckland (he made 54 in England's one innings), it was tempered by having to miss the last two days of that match because he had scratched the cornea of his right eye.

Thus, Bob Willis, doubtless unaware that it was a harbinger of the shape of things to come took the helm and Boycott's second and last tour of New Zealand ended as dismally as his first had done eleven years previously. Moreover, it could be said that his comeback was well and truly over. Good scores in Pakistan had consolidated the Test return but in New Zealand his hold on his place had been weakened. Boycott would once again have to fight his way back into the England team and, following an early-season injury in England, it would take him a surprisingly long time.

Averages for 1977–78 Series v New Zealand

Tests	I	NO	Runs	HS	Avge
3	5	0	166	77	33.20

Bowling: **Centuries:** 0
Fielding: 2   **Half-Centuries:** 2

Cumulative Test Career Averages

Tests	I	NO	Runs	HS	Avge
72	125	17	5,516	246*	51.07

Bowling: 127–36–350–7   **Centuries:** 15
Fielding: 22   **Half-Centuries:** 32

From a possible six Test appearances in the summer of 1978, three each against Pakistan and New Zealand, Boycott was able to make only two. In the first instance, injury caused the absence; on 25 May, whilst fielding in the first of the Prudential One-Day games against Pakistan, Boycott damaged his thumb. The injury was sufficiently troublesome to keep him out of the first and second Tests of the main Pakistan series and although he was back playing first-class cricket well in time for the third Test, he was not considered for the game by the selectors. Indeed it was not until the second Test at Trent Bridge, the scene of his emotional return one year earlier, that Boycott was able to regain his place. In a remarkable combination of circumstances, the setting, the action and Boycott's personal fortunes became a carbon copy of what had taken place twelve months previously against Australia.

With England batting first, Boycott had but 2 runs to his name when he was dropped by Geoff Howarth at third slip off Richard Hadlee. Uncannily, the unfortunate Howarth was standing in the same position as Rick McCosker had stood in 1977 when he also dropped Boycott. The result then had been a century. In 1978 it was the same although, strangely, there was a difference of sorts. Back in 1967 Boycott had been dropped from England's team for scoring 106* on the first day of a Test Match against India. Eleven years later he made 108 versus New

Zealand in the same period of time but, although the scores were nearly identical, there was no murmur of disapproval made.

In addition to having Boycott dropped, the hostile Hadlee gave him numerous other problems with which to contend before the battle was finally played out. Twice Boycott was perilously close to being lbw and so accurate was the bowling that it took him three hours and twenty minutes to reach his half-century. During the innings he received good support. There was an opening stand with Gooch (55) of 111 runs, followed by a second-wicket partnership of 129 runs with Clive Radley (59) and by the close of play Boycott and England were both well placed with the scoreboard reading 252 for 2. Boycott took his score on to 131 in fifty-five minutes play on the second morning.

It was at that juncture that Hadlee (he ended the England innings with figures of 42–11–94–4) gained a measure of revenge over Boycott. He fired two bouncers at the Yorkshireman. The first was hooked imperiously for 4 but the second found the top edge as Boycott played the stroke slightly out of position. The ball flew high into the air, eventually descending into the area of mid-on and Hadlee himself was stationed underneath it to claim the catch. He had bowled his heart out for more than a day and he had no intention of allowing anybody else near the catch!

New Zealand could not match England's 429 all out. Scores of 120 and 190 all out left them 119 runs short of making England bat again and the defeat in the final Test, which completed a 3–0 England whitewash, was no less emphatic, being by the decisive margin of 7 wickets. In this Test Boycott slowly worked his way in the first innings to 24, in a dour stand of 64 runs for the second wicket with Radley, after Gooch had fallen to the second ball of the innings. Hadlee was once more partly responsible for Boycott's downfall, holding a catch off the bowling of the eighteen-year-old Brendan Bracewell. In the second innings Hadlee's involvement was total. He bowled Boycott for 4 with a sizzling, slanting delivery that beat the Yorkshireman for speed as comprehensively as ever he had been.

Such deliveries stand out. It proved that Hadlee, when he put in a 'fast one', could produce the ball at a searing pace. Similarly Michael Holding, in the West Indies on the 1980–1 tour, who believed in letting an opening batsman have a really fast delivery right at the very beginning of his innings (which is not particularly easy for a bowler to achieve in his first over), produced one at Bridgetown that flashed through Boycott almost before he had time to lift his bat. Hadlee's delivery was not a one-off fluke. He repeated the deed with his very next delivery when Radley followed Boycott back to the pavilion as bewildered as his recently departed colleague.

The confrontation between Boycott and Hadlee, two masters of their respective trades, was a highlight of the series. With the former's century counterbalanced by the latter's two dismissals, plus his catch off Bracewell, in the two Tests in which they met, an honourable draw was a fair result. Of more personal interest was Boycott's Test aggregate. He was now realistically set to pass Sobers' record. At the end of the 1978 home season his aggregate stood at 5,675 runs which was still more than 2,000 runs short of his target. It was imperative for him, therefore, to pass figures such as the 6,000 mark as quickly as possible. It would be one more psychological barrier out of the way; and with six Tests due in Australia in 1978–9 there was every chance that that obstacle could be soon surmounted. But it was not to be. In view of what lay in store for Boycott between the end of the New Zealand series and the start of the Australian tour it was surprising that he scored any Test runs at all in Australia.

The flames of conflict were also now being fanned in earnest within Yorkshire; with Boycott inevitably at the centre of controversy. The long-simmering feud between himself, the Committee and various other Members would finally burst into the open.

Averages for 1978 Series v New Zealand

Tests	I	NO	Runs	HS	Avge
2	3	0	159	131	53.00

Bowling: Centuries: 1

Fielding: 0   Half-Centuries: 0

Cumulative Test Career Averages

Tests	I	NO	Runs	HS	Avge
74	128	17	5,675	246*	51.12

Bowling: 127–36–350–7   Centuries: 16

Fielding: 22   Half-Centuries: 32

11 In the wake of strife

What had slowly been rising to a boiling point over a period of seasons, without becoming headline news, suddenly spilled over into open hostility late in 1978. At long last the story of Geoffrey Boycott's relationship with both his fellow county players and the Yorkshire Club was coming to a head. At the end of September 1978, Boycott was relieved of the county captaincy. That, in a nutshell, was as much as took place but two months before the decision was taken it had become public knowledge that there was a deep rift between the captain and his players and, to make matters worse, the split was broadcast outside the county in the most demonstrative manner possible.

Yorkshire was playing Northamptonshire at Northampton in the County Championship, although as the match progressed it became increasingly difficult to judge who was opposing whom. In the first innings Boycott scored 113 runs but in the process he occupied the crease for 90 out of the 100 overs available. In direct protest at this virtual one run per over rate of scoring, Jackie Hampshire and Colin Johnson in the remaining 10 overs scored 11 runs, and spurned the opportunity of going for an extra batting bonus point. The press was quick to point out Hampshire's action, or lack of it, the following day.

Hampshire was summoned to appear in front of the Yorkshire Committee who not only disciplined him for his 'go slow' but threatened him with dismissal if the action was repeated. This was difficult to reconcile with subsequent events, for, following Boycott's demotion from captaincy, it was Hampshire himself who was invited to take over. Perhaps, after all it was not so strange. The Committee had also recently appointed Raymond Illingworth as general manager for the next season, 1979. He had left Yorkshire nearly a decade earlier (wanting, but not obtaining, the security of a contract of more than one season's duration) and he left to play with Leicestershire. The rights or wrongs of the decisions and appointments made were of less importance than the bewildering incompatibility of successive actions.

Consequently, the furore over Boycott's sacking as captain was not going to melt away. The clamour from around the county was instantaneous and it was not simply over the firing of Boycott from the captaincy. The manner of the dismissal left a great deal to be desired. The

Yorkshire Club announced the decision in the same week that the news was broken Boycott had suffered the loss of his mother, with whom he lived. There appeared to be precious little thought given to this bereavement or to Boycott's feelings.

Naturally, the press and media could not make enough of the sensation. Boycott had already lost the vice-captaincy of England to Bob Willis for the next Australian tour. Now, he could even have lost not just the captaincy of his county, but his very club. There was no precedent in the twentieth century in Yorkshire cricket of a deposed captain continuing to play in the county side and it was against this background of uncertainty and insecurity that Boycott had to go to Australia. However, long before the tour began Boycott made a fightback. Unfortunately, it was probably his biggest mistake.

Immediately after it was made public that Boycott was no longer Yorkshire's captain he appeared on the Michael Parkinson Show on BBC Television. It was all well and good to 'state his case', but it was a major upheaval in his career and a very traumatic and testing time for him. Having lost both the England vice-captaincy and the Yorkshire captaincy, Boycott must have felt the whole world was against him. Yet, going on to Parkinson's show was bound to cause hostility, no matter what he said, but it was particularly true in an aspect that was not much noticed at the time.

Boycott had a genuine grievance to air towards the Yorkshire Committee concerning their insensitivity towards his bereavement. Unfortunately, when talking to Parkinson, Boycott was not content to restrict his comments to his own personal issue. For a lengthy part of the chat Boycott went into great detail of how, when England pace bowler Chris Old had similarly lost a parent, his father, during a county game, Boycott had bent over backwards to see that Old was released from the game in which he was playing and went straight home to his family.

On that point, there is no reason to doubt that Boycott was as helpful and as understanding as he could have been. Similarly, there was no reciprocation by the Yorkshire Committee when Boycott was in a similar position, *but* he should not have allowed his feelings on the matter to drag Old's grief into his discussion with Parkinson. It was a comparison in the worst possible taste. If Boycott had stuck to his own inside rail he would have won the race against the Committee without breaking sweat. Instead, by referring directly to Old, he probably lost more friends than he won.

However, when Old himself became Yorkshire captain the famous poll, which he conducted amongst the players to see how many players would prefer to play in a Yorkshire side that was minus Boycott, became a serious bone of contention with the club. That poll too may have been wrong and Old was heavily criticised for conducting it but there was one good reason why it happened, and the blame did not lie entirely with Old.

In the light of all that had happened in such a short space of time it is difficult to imagine how Boycott could concentrate fully on the six-Test series that was looming ahead in Australia. Yet, despite all the upheavals, protests and behind-the-scenes arguments which occurred during 1978, the English season had still been quite successful for him. He scored 1,233 runs at an average of 51.37 and hit six centuries, but the Australian tour, in the wake of so much strife, was almost a complete disaster for him. Boycott's average for the tour was only 26.65 per innings but the figure does not tell the true story. He was obviously in no fit state to tour.

Perhaps it would have been better for Boycott to have stayed at home but that could have had the opposite effect, and playing cricket, even if not playing very well, may have been the better therapy in the long run. There were certainly no lasting effects caused by his dramatic experiences in late 1978. Boycott returned from Australia to pick up the threads and play a splendid series against India at home. If nothing else, that spoke wonderfully well for the man's resilience. Alone, and especially in the context of 1978–9, it is worthy of the utmost admiration.

Averages for 1978–79 Series v Australia

Tests	I	NO	Runs	HS	Avge
6	12	0	263	77	21.92

Bowling: 1–0–6–0   **Centuries:** 0

Fielding: 2   **Half-Centuries:** 1

Cumulative Test Career Averages

Tests	I	NO	Runs	HS	Avge
80	140	17	5,938	246*	48.27

Bowling: 128–36–356–7   **Centuries:** 16

Fielding: 24   **Half-Centuries:** 33

The Australian tour and its aftermath gave to Boycott a strange double-edged situation full of conflicting ironies. In the first instance, England trounced Australia by five victories to one, the heaviest defeat ever inflicted upon them by their oldest enemy, but apart from one innings of 77 in the second Test, Boycott's contribution to the 1978–9 series was negligible. Yet, he returned to English domestic cricket to record an average of 102.53 per innings for the 1979 season (1,538 runs from twenty innings). He repeated his feat of 1971 when he became the first Englishman to average more than 100 in all games of a first-class season. In the context of what had transpired in 1978 and 1979 the latter performance was quite staggering. In 1971 Boycott had been at the very height of his powers, whereas 1979 had been prefaced by a winter that contained sufficient setbacks to finish many players. But not Boycott.

He scored six centuries in 1979 and into the bargain passed his 6,000th Test run, that milestone being reached in the first Test of the summer.

The Test series in 1979 was against India and it turned into a strange affair. Due to the staging of the second World Cup one-day competition the series was reduced to four matches, and then various factors combined to limit Boycott's possible eight innings to only five. Nevertheless, Boycott scored 378 runs in the series, including two centuries, but after winning the first Test with ridiculous ease, England never again appeared to have the edge over India who also possessed a batsman capable of eclipsing all others from both teams. That player was Sunil Gavaskar whose greatest moment came in the final Test, after Boycott had already scored his two centuries, 155 and 125 at Edgbaston and The Oval respectively. However, by the time the Oval Test had ended it was clear that a batsman had emerged who could not only rival Boycott as an opener but actually surpass him.

If the 1979 series were to be judged in terms of a race between Boycott and Gavaskar, the Indian won by a furlong but it was Boycott who made the running throughout the summer until the last innings of the series. Then Gavaskar produced a surge and in the process took India to the very brink of what would have been one of the most stunning victories in Test cricket. No less a judge than Sir Leonard Hutton rated Gavaskar's 221 as one of the three best Test double centuries he had ever witnessed.

Long before the Oval Test Boycott had used his limited opportunities extremely well. In each of the first three Tests he batted just once with the first Test at Edgbaston being his best innings. Brearley took first innings on winning the toss and not until 426 runs were on the board was Boycott dismissed, at which point he had 155 runs to his name after having shared in two very large partnerships with Graham Gooch and David Gower. Initially, the early batting had been scrappy. An opening stand of 66 contained as many as twenty-four extras and that latter figure occurred again when Randall replaced Brearley. Two dozen were added before the Nottinghamshire man departed; then Gooch strode to the wicket to give the game the kiss of life. In a matter of two hours he and Boycott added 145 runs for the third wicket with Gooch leading the charge by smiting one six and thirteen other boundaries in his innings of 83.

After the dismissal of Gooch, David Gower stayed with Boycott until the end of the first day when the score stood at 318 for 3 wickets, out of which Boycott had contributed 113* and Gower 43*. On the morrow they took their stand to 191 for the fourth wicket before Boycott fell leg-before to Kapil Dev. First blood to the Yorkshireman, and with Gower going on to complete a not out 200, Brearley was able to declare at 633 for 5, ninety minutes from the close of the second day, which set India a tremendous task to save the game. Averting the follow-on would have been quite an achievement but despite Gavaskar (61) and Vishwanath (78) both batting comfortably until the former, crazily attempted to beat Randall's arm, India capitulated some 336 runs behind the England total. Gavaskar again batted soundly in the second innings, sharing in a stand of 124 for the first wicket with Chetan Chauhan. He made 68 but from a score of 227 for 4 the Indians crashed to 253 all out to give England victory by an innings and 83 runs. Botham was the destroyer, taking 4 for 10 in 5 overs and the last 6 wickets fell for 26 runs in the space of 10.1 overs.

At Lord's, in the second Test, India were again in trouble until a huge third wicket stand of 210 runs by Vengsarkar and Vishwanath in the second innings blunted England's attack for more than five hours. England's batsmen accumulated 419 for 9 declared without the aid of a century. Boycott's share was 32 before he was caught in the gully off Ghavri by Gavaskar. Although the Indians had again to follow-on, after being bowled out for 96 at the first time of asking, the two centurions, Vishwanath and Vengsarkar, carried the visitors to safety.

Thence to Leeds and another drawn Test, where the loss of more than eleven hours playing allowed less than two full innings to be completed. It was cruel luck on the Indians for they dismissed England for a modest 270 runs (Boycott making 31), but as the innings was not completed until the fourth day the Indians could make no capital from the situation. In fact, the only interest when India batted was whether or not Gavaskar would finally reach the century he had already four times threatened to score in the series but failed to reach. He also failed at the fifth attempt for, after reaching 78 quite effortlessly, Gavaskar was teased out by a beautifully flighted delivery from Edmonds which crept underneath his bat and bowled him. Even so, after scores of 61, 68, 42, 59 and 78, Gavaskar could justifiably hope for better things at The Oval.

The sequence of events there once again placed Boycott in the forefront of the action. England had batted first with Boycott falling lbw to Kapil Dev for 35. England made 305 all out and removed India for 202 to take an apparently commanding lead and Gavaskar's 13 in that innings was his one real failure of the entire series. When Boycott scored 125 in England's second innings, it appeared to be game, set and match to the Yorkshireman. He was opening the English second innings by lunch on the third day and stayed at the crease for seven hours despite having to bat for most of the Monday with back trouble. It was a fine performance, and he was eventually bowled behind his legs by Ghavri, misjudging the line of the ball. When Brearley declared at 334 for 8 late on the fourth day India appeared to be beaten, for their target was an 'impossible' 438 to win. But Gavaskar and Chauhan saw the matter in a completely different light.

By the close of play on that penultimate day the pair had taken the score to 76. On the last day that opening partnership stretched to 213 runs. Then Chauhan was caught in the slips for 80 but Gavaskar was playing the innings of his life. The final result, with India failing by just 9 runs to reach that seemingly 'impossible' 438 runs, has been well documented, but for Boycott the drama held a more poignant significance. He had been outgunned by Gavaskar.

When Gavaskar came to England with his tremendous world record breaking reputation in 1979 there had always been, to some, the nagging doubt that he had failed to turn on the tap in England. At The Oval that myth was shattered. Gavaskar scored 221 runs, and the sight of him pouring cooling water on to his arms during each drinks interval before returning to the fray was one which became etched on the minds of millions of television viewers. It displayed a relish for the task ahead that upstaged even Boycott at the best. Gavaskar was, and still is, the sole batsman to make a century in both innings of the same Test on three separate occasions. All three feats were accomplished before the 1979 series yet when he arrived in England there were still those who placed him behind Boycott because Gavaskar had scored but one Test hundred in England. That one innings of 221 runs was sufficient to prove the detractors wrong.

At The Oval in 1979 Boycott recorded his eighteenth Test century by scoring 125 in his eighty-fourth Test Match and 145th Test innings. Gavaskar's 221 was his *twentieth* three-figure Test score, made in his *fiftieth* Test Match and only his *ninety-third* Test innings. By any standards, even considering perhaps the wickets more favourable to run-getting in the hotter countries, and quite apart from Gavaskar's other world Test records, that put him some way ahead of Boycott.

Averages for 1979 Series v India

Tests	I	NO	Runs	HS	Avge
4	5	0	378	155	75.60

Bowling: 7–3–8–0   **Centuries:** 2
Fielding: 1   **Half-Centuries:** 0

Cumulative Test Career Averages

Tests	I	NO	Runs	HS	Avge
84	145	17	6,316	246*	49.34

Bowling: 135–39–364–7   **Centuries:** 18
Fielding: 25   **Half-Centuries:** 33

Due principally to financial considerations, England went to Australia for the second winter in succession in 1979–80 and, once again, Boycott enjoyed contrasting fortune. He was much more successful in 1979–80 but Australia, strengthened by the return of their Packer players, thrashed England 3–0 to recoup some of their pride, if not the Ashes, following their 5–1 humiliation in the previous series. The West Indies were in Australia at the same time as England to play a three-way one-day series which meant there was no time for a normal five- or six-Test series. However, there was to be one extra Test to be played by England. On their way home from Australia the team stopped at Bombay to play a Jubilee Test against India to mark the fiftieth anniversary of the founding of the Indian Board of Cricket Control. Thus, Boycott made his first visit to India to complement his similar excursion to Pakistan some two years earlier.

Therefore, on the full tour there were eight first-class games, including the Tests, as well as a plethora of one-day games. Outside of the Tests there was one century, 110 versus South Australia at Adelaide, and Boycott played in all but one of the first-class matches on the tour. The first Test at Perth was probably his best game, despite falling lbw to Lillee for 0 in the first innings. Initially, Brearley had put Australia in to bat, but history did not seem to favour this action since England had not won a Test in Australia in this manner since 1912, at Melbourne. Defeat, indeed, duly followed by 138 runs although it was not before a sterling performance from Boycott. Following his first innings 0, he strove desperately to salvage a draw for England after Australia had offered a target of 354 runs to win in one full day plus sixty-five minutes.

Boycott scored 99*, batting for practically all of the last day, but with 14.4 overs of the mandatory final twenty overs remaining Bob Willis was caught by Greg Chappell off Geoff Dymock to clinch the Australian victory. Ironically, Willis was also dismissed in the second Test when David Gower was 98* – not an enviable double. Nor did the tale of missed centuries end there. Greg Chappell completed the match also on 98* when Australia won by 6 wickets although Ian Botham sportingly gave Chappell his chance by purposely serving up a rank long hop for him to attempt to finish the game with a six and so reach his hundred. In this game Boycott registered scores of 8 and 18, but in the third Test at Melbourne, notwithstanding another heavy defeat by 8 wickets, he returned to form.

With Graham Gooch as his partner Boycott (44) put up 116 runs for the first wicket of the first innings. It was the highest opening stand for England since the same pair had scored 111 against New Zealand at Trent Bridge in 1978. Unfortunately, with the Australians cruising to victory in the last session of the match the only prospect remaining was for some reward against India in Bombay as the tour drew to a close.

As England gained a 10-wicket victory at the expense of India the tour did end on a brighter note and it did so for Boycott too who scored 43* in the second innings as he and Gooch ambled their way towards the 98 runs required. The game was completely dominated by a brilliant all round performance from Ian Botham (a century and 13 wickets in the match) and some great wicketkeeping from Bob Taylor (ten catches in the match, seven in the first innings) which gave him a world Test record. As if that were not enough the same pair shared a record sixth wicket stand of 171 runs, the highest for that wicket in Anglo–Indian Tests. Therefore, considering the joint contributions of Botham and Taylor, Boycott (43*) and Gooch (49*) performed rather well to salvage some personal glory for themselves in the final run-chase. After the disappointments in Australia the 10-wicket win, achieved in four days, was a welcome tonic before returning home. Less heartening was the prospect that awaited England in the coming season.

Averages for 1979–80 Series v Australia

Tests	I	NO	Runs	HS	Avge
3	6	1	176	99*	35.20

Bowling: **Centuries:** 0
Fielding: 2   **Half-Centuries:** 1

Jubilee Test in India 1979–80

Tests	I	NO	Runs	HS	Avge
1	2	1	65	43*	65.00

Bowling: **Centuries:** 0
Fielding: 0   **Half-Centuries:** 0

Cumulative Test Career Averages

Tests	I	NO	Runs	HS	Avge
88	153	19	6,557	246*	48.93

Bowling: 135–39–364–7   **Centuries:** 18
Fielding: 27   **Half-Centuries:** 34

12 West Indies all the way

When the 1980 series against the West Indies began Boycott was a little less than 1,500 runs short of Sir Garfield Sobers' world Test aggregate record of 8,032 runs. However, although Boycott's personal tally in Test cricket had risen to 6,557 runs he was not only still some way short of Sobers' record but even of Colin Cowdrey's English Test record aggregate of 7,624 runs. In fact, before the first Test of 1980 Boycott stood at number seven in the pecking-order of all time Test run-scorers behind Sobers, Cowdrey, Hammond (7,249 runs), Bradman (6,996), Hutton (6,971) and Barrington (6,806). Even so the goal was now within sight and range.

As the world record drew nearer, however, it was becoming clear that Test Match runs were becoming more difficult for Boycott to accrue than in the past. Thus, while his undoubted class as a batsman always shone through he was no longer the potent Test Match force of yesteryear.

An example of the gradual decline of Boycott's powers at Test level was his inability to attain centuries in international games with the regularity that had once been taken for granted. There were no centuries at all in the 1980 series against the West Indies (although it is fair to point out how strong was the West Indies attack) and while he did score a hundred in the Centenary Test played at Lord's at the end of the season against Australia it scarcely held the same significance as many of the hundreds he had scored in other Tests. The innings was played at a time when the match was already dying a slow death and there was no possibility of a definite result. Notwithstanding, of far greater importance was the fact that that particular innings was the twentieth in Tests played by him since his last recorded Test century, his 125 versus India at The Oval. This compared to his career average of a century in every eighth Test innings.

The series against the West Indies (for all its 368 Boycott runs at an average of 40.88) could not be rated as a success. The West Indies won by 1–0 with four Tests drawn. Ian Botham also had an inauspicious debut as England's captain. For Boycott, the elevation of Botham to the captaincy must surely have been a very bitter pill to swallow. It was almost as if anybody but Boycott could have the job. That is no slight on Botham. He was not ready for the job and should never have been given it. Botham was a great all-round cricketer but he was still inexperienced, and anyway the best players do not necessarily make the best leaders. But simply in giving Botham the captaincy the selectors were stating categorically, by gesture if not by word of mouth, that the place at England's helm would never again be Boycott's. After losing the vice-captaincy to Willis two years earlier this was always on the cards. Now it was official. Oh, how Boycott paid for that defeat in Wellington in 1978 versus New Zealand!

Fortunately, in a drab 1980 summer there were some bonus points to offset Boycott's disappointment. Mainly they came in his 558 Test runs scored off the West Indian and Australian attacks which took him to new heights in the record books. But this failed to dispel the clouds of defeat that hovered over the England team.

Due primarily to the weather, the opening match proved to be the decisive Test of the rubber. The West Indies won at Trent Bridge by the narrow margin of 2 wickets. Botham won the toss and elected to bat, but when Boycott had scored only 4 he was dropped by Deryck Murray behind the stumps. With the match's decidedly close finish such a miss could have been extremely costly. Murray was very much a contemporary of Boycott for he had begun his Test career a full year before Boycott, also in England, and this particular tour was to be his swansong in international cricket. By way of atoning for his earlier lapse Murray safely clasped a second chance offered by Boycott, from the bowling of Garner, when he had advanced to 36. For added good measure, he was to do so twice again before the series ended.

When stumps were drawn on the first day six more batsmen had joined Boycott in the pavilion while 243 runs were scored. This total was increased by only 20 runs on the second morning, and this spiritless capitulation gave the West Indies a splendid opportunity to establish a commanding lead. Surprisingly, it did not materialise. A final total of 308 all out was only 45 runs ahead. On the third morning, therefore, Boycott and Gooch had, on paper, a much easier task ahead of them than had been expected.

The Yorkshire–Essex pair put on 46 runs to take England fractionally ahead of their visitors. At that total Gooch was run out by the sparkling Faoud Bacchus and at 68 Boycott lost his second partner, Chris Tavare. Consequently, it was left to another veteran, Bob Woolmer, to stay with Boycott if England were to compile a respectable second innings total. They both performed admirably. With patient determination the two senior players added 106 runs for the third wicket. In total, Boycott stayed at the crease for more than five hours but despite the slow scoring, England's position would have been parlous without their efforts.

Whenever Boycott batted slowly criticism was levelled at him. Yet at Trent Bridge he and Woolmer were all that stood between the West

Indies and victory. Once the pair was parted (they were dismissed within minutes of each other, Boycott being bowled by Roberts for 75 and Woolmer made 29) the England innings disintegrated from 174 for 3 to 252 all out. This left the West Indies an apparently simple task. They required 208 runs for victory with more than eight hours playing time at their disposal. Furthermore, by close of play on the fourth day the West Indies needed only 92 more runs on the morrow with 8 of their second innings wickets still intact.

The irrepressible Bob Willis, however, tore into the West Indies batting to such effect on the last day that he almost snatched an amazing victory for England. He scythed through the middle order to take 5 for 65 in an inspired spell of bowling and only Desmond Haynes was able to withstand the bombardment.

Haynes defiantly battled his way to 62 before being run out when within three runs of clinching the win practically off his own bat. Although there were but 2 wickets remaining at that stage England were unable to hammer home those final nails to take a memorable triumph from the very jaws of defeat. A tremendous Test Match ended, therefore, amid high drama with the West Indies taking the honours by the skin of their teeth.

After Nottingham there was a slight air of anti-climax. The series floated along to each of the four other venues, amidst a continuous catalogue of rain, bad light and more rain. At Lord's, more than eight hours were lost in the first two days; at Old Trafford ten-and-a-half hours went astray; next, a full day disappeared at The Oval and at Leeds, for the third successive year, the Test was a virtual wash-out. All of the first and third days were taken by the rain, plus half of the second day; but, despite the wholesale takeover by the elements, the West Indies were still able to assert a chilling superiority over England. The Tests were barely true contests because of the drastic shortage of playing time, yet in every game the West Indies succeeded in making England bat twice to their once. Perhaps it was as well that the weather did intervene.

However, there were a few grains of satisfaction to be gleaned by Boycott. To follow his second innings 75 at Trent Bridge he made two further notable contributions. The first was 86 in the third Test at Old Trafford. It occurred also in the second innings following an abysmal first innings when England was put out for 150. With the West Indies taking a lead of 110 runs Boycott's second effort, along with a similar performance by Peter Willey, who made 62*, undoubtedly saved England. Boycott batted long enough to thwart a breakthrough by the West Indies until he fell leg-before to Holding early on the last morning. Willey then took charge until stumps were drawn from a rather precarious position of being only 180 runs ahead with just three hours play and four English wickets remaining. The draw was thus gained, but of more surprise was that the game had produced the first drawn Test at Manchester between England and the West Indies since 1955 – twenty-five years and seven tours earlier.

Unusually, The Oval staged the fourth Test instead of the traditional final match (because of the Centenary Test at Lord's against Australia some weeks later) and while Boycott showed exemplary courage the game was also a very painful exercise for him to undertake. The fearsome West Indian battery of fast bowlers put into practice a theory that Boycott was vulnerable to quick bowling from around the wicket. Presumably by bowling right-arm-round, and rather short, the ball that slanted across Boycott would have him fencing outside the off-stump. While the tactic was legitimate it was also negative and at The Oval it was positively dangerous. One ball from Croft rose steeply, hit Boycott's arm, rocketed onwards and upwards into his visor, drew blood from above his right eyebrow and eventually gave him two very black eyes.

The injury was sustained in the first innings and Boycott was forced to retire hurt. He returned at the fall of the first wicket at 155, to continue his innings pluckily to 53 before he was brilliantly run out by Greenidge from mid-on. In this match England took a substantial first innings lead over the West Indies but the third day went the same way as so many other days in the series and no clear result could be produced.

With Headingley washed away, Boycott's Test runs from the series became academic too. His aggregate had now advanced to 6,925 at 48.42 per innings, and with the forthcoming Test versus Australia presenting a possible two more innings for Boycott, the question was, in the minds of his followers and cricket statisticians alike, would he reach 7,000 runs in that match?

Averages for 1980 Series v West Indies

Tests	I	NO	Runs	HS	Avge
5	10	1	368	86	40.88

Bowling: 7–2–11–0   Centuries: 0
Fielding: 0   Half-Centuries: 3

Centenary Test v Australia 1980

Tests	I	NO	Runs	HS	Avge
1	2	1	190	128*	190.00

Bowling: Centuries: 1
Fielding: 0   Half-Centuries: 1

Cumulative Test Career Averages

Tests	I	NO	Runs	HS	Avge
94	165	21	7,115	246*	49.40

Bowling: 142–41–375–7   Centuries: 19
Fielding: 27   Half-Centuries: 38

The Centenary Test was as badly affected by the weather as all of the earlier Tests of the summer. In the first three days at Lord's almost ten hours playing time was forfeited and, as a result, Australia batted until late on the third evening before declaring their first innings closed. Despite Graham Wood making 112 it was Kim Hughes who stole the limelight. His improvisation brought fourteen fours and three sixes during an innings of the highest class. It took Australia to 385 for 5 and when England replied, Boycott with 62 was the sole home player to pass 50. Lillee and Pascoe caused the damage, bowling out England for 205 runs long before the fourth day was over; which gave Australia time to extend their lead to 286 runs by reaching 106 for 2 by the close of play.

On the final day, Australia hit up 83 runs in less than an hour before declaring at 189 for 4 to set England an unlikely target of 370 runs to win in six hours. Hughes was outstanding. He made 84 and was desperately unlucky not to record his second century of the Test. He performed quite magnificently in both innings but of all his startlingly powerful strokes, the finest was the kind of stroke an ageing grandfather would recount to his children's children. Facing Chris Old, the Yorkshire fast bowler, Hughes strode down the wicket to meet him with the elegance of a Nureyev at Covent Garden and then, with the majestic power of an Olympic javelin thrower, disdainfully hoisted the ball on to the top of the Lord's pavilion – it was an awesome hit, the like of which had only rarely been witnessed in the past.

As for Boycott, he remained less flamboyant and as phlegmatic as ever. Once he had lost Gooch and Athey before 50 was on the board, safety beckoned him. Consequently, he stayed at the crease for the rest of the day calmly assisting England to meander to 244 for 3 wickets. The result, apart from the game being drawn, was another Boycott century, 128*, which also took him past a number of personal milestones. During the innings he passed the Test aggregates of Sir Leonard Hutton (6,971) and Sir Donald Bradman (6,996), took his own Test tally beyond 7,000 (to 7,115), scored his sixth Test century against Australia and, finally, his nineteenth in all Tests. It was an impressive performance; unfortunately, it did not have the flair or dexterity of Hughes' two innings and the Australian was worthily made 'Man of the Match'.

On a more mundane level, the century versus Australia was only the second three-figure score of the season for Boycott. The first, unusually, had not materialised until as late as August, thus emphasising a generally barren year around the counties. He had taken 135 off Lancashire, following which came the Lord's Test, and then Boycott caned Derbyshire for 154* at Scarborough in September. However, only three centuries for an entire season was a most un-Boycott-like state of affairs.

One had to retrace Boycott's statistics for more than a decade to find a parallel parlous scarcity of centuries. In 1965, for the only time in his career, he failed to score a hundred in first-class matches in England but, apart from that year, only in 1963 and 1969 had he made as few as three centuries in a full season. Admittedly the weather was a major factor. However, if any county bowlers thought that Boycott's spirit was sagging, 1981 was to see a slight improvement and by 1982 and 1983, Boycott was back to his previous prolific form. There was still plenty of cricket left in him! England's tour of the West Indies in 1980–1 followed hard upon the series in England. Unfortunately, it was an extremely poor tour for all concerned.

Boycott was making his third, and almost certainly his last, Test visit to the Caribbean. In comparison to the two previous tours, and in relation to his own standards, his later performances rarely rose higher than average. He played in every first-class fixture on the trip but his aggregate of 818 runs from seventeen innings in nine games was well below his performance in 1967–8 (1,154 runs from eleven games and sixteen innings) and 1973–4 (960 runs from ten games and sixteen innings). In mitigation, there were the numerous morale sapping problems that the tour had continually to surmount. None of the players remained unaffected by the sequence of events, especially the Robin Jackman affair and the sad death of Ken Barrington during one of the Test Matches, which particularly cut at the heart of the English tourists.

It was not surprising that England lost the series. Proceedings began dismally in the first Test at Port-of-Spain with a resounding defeat by an innings and 79 runs, in the wake of which came the Jackman affair in Guyana. Due to Jackman's connections with South Africa (he had played there, had business interests there, and also was married to a South African) the authorities saw fit to refuse him entry to Guyana and this led to the cancellation of the second Test, and nearly the rest of the tour. The move was blatantly political. If Jackman was not welcome in Guyana, the government could have made the fact plain as soon as it was clear that the England squad was to be reinforced by Jackman (he replaced Willis, who had to fly home for a knee operation).

From Guyana the players went on to Bridgetown where there was another heavy defeat, by 298 runs, and with the remaining two Tests ending drawn the world champions cruised to a 2–0 victory in the series. From it all, Boycott emerged with a very mixed bag of scores from the four Tests. In sequence he made 30, 70, 0, 1, 38, 104*, 40 and 12. Of those innings only two out of eight bore any real significance, although the 0, in its own strange way, was not without a share of superb dramatic appeal.

The innings of 70 came in the second innings of the first Test, after England had followed on 248 runs behind the West Indies first innings score of 426 for 9 declared. Due to rain taking away more than a full day's play, some eight hours and forty-five minutes remained when England began the task of saving the game and Boycott, with his 70 runs, made every effort to be there until the bitter end. Not until five others had preceded him to the dressing-room was Boycott dismissed, more than five hours after first taking guard. There was only a draw to play for and Boycott was the ideal person for the job. But once he had departed, the West Indies did not loosen the stranglehold his dismissal had given them on the game.

The century likewise occurred in the second innings of a Test, the fourth at Antigua which was also the inaugural Test on that island's St John's ground. Batting first, England made 271 all out but, notwithstanding rain which claimed all of the fourth day, by the start of the final day they faced a deficit of 190 runs with all second innings wickets intact. Defeat was distinctly possible. However, on this occasion Boycott did stay at the crease until the very end and thus 'saved' England yet again, although with Gooch making 83 out of an opening partnership of 144 runs it was not all Boycott's own work. On the other side of the coin, what was Boycott's own, namely his innings of 104*, was all the more memorable. It took five hours and forty-five minutes to compile and contained nine boundaries, was Boycott's twentieth Test hundred, and his 121st in all first-class cricket. Coupled with his first innings 38 which had taken him past Hammond's Test aggregate of 7,249 runs, it sealed Boycott's best performance of the series.

In between the scores of 70 and 104* there had been another quite different event in the third Test at Bridgetown in March 1981; namely, a Boycott 'duck', but it was no ordinary 0. There was no indiscretion or lapse of concentration on his part. Boycott was unfortunate enough to encounter, momentarily, fast bowling perfection from Michael Holding.

It was a moment of pure magic, a rare flash in time when everything slotted perfectly into place to make him the superb athlete serving delivery after delivery with all the grace and elegance of a gazelle in beautiful motion but with the ravenous venom of a tiger tearing into its prey. In human terms for Boycott it constituted a full over of uninterrupted torture that culminated with an executionary delivery which left Boycott numbed and shellshocked. In days gone by the legendary F. R. Spofforth had had his 'judgement' ball. This, surely, was its modern-day equivalent.

The action took place in the second over of the England first innings after Graham Gooch had played through the opening over from Andy Roberts. From the outset, Gooch and Boycott were wary because the pitch was not as perfect as the best Test Match strips. The West Indies had made no more than 265 all out on it, but with Holding in his prevailing mood it probably made little difference how the pitch was playing. His first ball to Boycott appeared to be offered at a shade above medium pace. However, at that stage of his career, Holding had a most disconcerting habit of letting an opener have an extra fast delivery right at the beginning of his innings. Consequently, each successive ball of that over to Boycott became appreciably quicker than the previous one as Holding strove to reach an electrifying climax. Boycott was obviously in trouble. He did not middle a single delivery but when the sixth ball of the over was hurtling towards him he could not touch even with a thin edge.

His bat, so often impregnable in the past, was still upraised as the ball flashed past Boycott at a tremendous velocity. It pitched only marginally short of the wickets and cut back to send the off-stump cartwheeling. Rarely, if ever, had Boycott been bowled by such a vicious delivery. He had encountered Holding, for the few minutes it took, at his most lithe, athletic, ferocious and terrifying best. Sheer speed beat Boycott, and that alone made Holding, on that day and for those precious fleeting moments, different from any other Test fast bowler in the world.

Away from the wicket, as a footnote to the episode, England's Chris Old stood on the pavilion balcony surveying the scene. It was said at the time that, on seeing Holding produce the execution ball, he gaped in stunned amazement. First, there was the savagery of Holding. Second, there was Boycott looking forlornly behind him at two stumps. As realisation dawned of precisely what he had witnessed, one near at hand commentator went so far as to say that a look of terror spread slowly across Old's countenance 'and he too (like Boycott) had the look of a man who had seen a monster'.

Some batsmen might have been shattered mentally by the after effects of such a confrontation, perhaps to the extent of a career at Test level being shattered. Certainly, a mental attitude, particularly that of Holding, played a considerable part in the drama. Holding 'psyched' himself up to deliver the 'coup de grâce' and he won the battle decisively, almost cruelly. Fortunately, Boycott was never one to retreat in the face of the enemy. Some critics have said that he did exactly that by opting out of Test cricket in the mid-1970s and thus avoiding Lillee and Thomson when they were terrorising English batsmen. Be that as it may, Boycott disproved the theory, in the West Indies at least, by hitting back with his undefeated century in the fourth Test. It was as well that he did. It gave his tour, if not England's, some semblance of respectability.

Averages for 1980–81 Series v West Indies

Tests	I	NO	Runs	HS	Avge
4	8	1	295	104*	42.14

Bowling: 3–2–5–0   **Centuries: 1**

Fielding: 2   **Half-Centuries: 1**

Cumulative Test Career Averages

Tests	I	NO	Runs	HS	Avge
98	173	22	7,410	246*	49.07

Bowling: 145–43–380–7   **Centuries: 20**

Fielding: 29   **Half-Centuries: 39**

13 A record to take home – straightaway

Sobers' Test aggregate record, the destination towards which Boycott was travelling, came closer with the 1981 season. Boycott now had 7,410 Test runs to his name. Between him and Sobers there was only Cowdrey, and by the end of the 1980–1 West Indian series the gap separating Boycott from Cowdrey had been narrowed to 214 runs. Therefore, it was more probable than otherwise that, with six Tests scheduled for that year against Australia, Boycott could expect to be embarking on the final leg of his journey long before the series was completed. In the event, what once would have been accomplished with relative ease in half-a-dozen innings or less now took him nearly twice as long.

The parallel that could be drawn between Boycott's batting against Australia and his earlier performances in the West Indies was striking. Only two innings out of eight played in the Caribbean had been of real substance. Similarly, the Australians found Boycott to be much less than his usual prolific self and, as if to emphasise that he was now past the zenith of his Test career, he fared even worse than he had on tour. In England, prior to the sixth Test, Boycott aggregated only 255 runs from ten innings at an average of 25.50. In the West Indies he had scored 295 runs from eight attempts at an average of 42.14. Even with his century in the sixth Test Boycott's final average of 32.66 for twelve innings against Australia in 1981 was almost as low as in any other full-length series in which he played during eighteen years of Test cricket. In 1966 he averaged 26.57 in four (out of five) Tests and seven innings when playing the West Indies at home. Many years later, in a six-Test series in Australia during 1978–9, he fell to 21.92 from twelve innings but the latter (as described in Chapter 11) was a series in which Boycott should never have participated. There were other averages of less than 30 but they came after three-Test series which cannot be taken in the same context as a full five- or six-Test series. Nevertheless, 1981 proved to be the third lowest series average of his career.

Not surprisingly, a lack of consistent contributions meant that there was not a great deal of Boycott-interest in the 1981 battle for the Ashes. It was also equally true that he was completely over-shadowed as a personality in the series by the events surrounding two other England players. Ian Botham's short period as England captain (he did not win a single Test in twelve attempts) culminated with a 'pair' in the second Test and his immediate resignation. This brought Mike Brearley back into the captaincy to pick up the pieces of a shattered team which had lost and drawn the first two Tests. Consequently, with Brearley and Botham holding the limelight and media-attention, the few episodes which revolved around Boycott were confined primarily to the second and sixth Tests.

Following scores of 27 and 4 in the 4-wicket defeat at Trent Bridge in the opening game, Boycott went to Lord's for the second Test on the threshold of another memorable milestone in his career. His one hundredth appearance for England placed Boycott in very select Test Match company. He was only the second man, after M. C. Cowdrey, to reach that distinguished achievement.

At Lord's the circumstances and conditions bore all the hallmarks of a Boycott success. For, by the time the England second innings began, late on the fourth day, the match was already set for a draw. England, with 311 all out, had a slight first innings deficit of 34 runs but there was barely time left to force a result. Boycott lost Gooch and Woolmer for the addition of 55 runs before Gower kept him company until the final day began and the pair then remained together while 123 runs were added for the third wicket. With Boycott in residence for four hours and thirty-nine minutes a century should have been the result, but after painstakingly compiling 60 runs, the combination of Marsh and Lillee brought his dismissal.

The end of this marathon effort, followed by the end of the match, was also the signal for the end of Ian Botham's reign as England's captain. He resigned after the game petered out to a draw.

Boycott too was ploughing a furrow that took him into the depths of cricketing despondency. In the following Tests he was completely out of touch although the restoration of Brearley to the leadership dramatically transformed the England team as a whole. A losing 1–0 position was magically fashioned into a winning 3–1 margin but it was not until the final sixth Test that Boycott showed form that was anything approaching his best. His efforts of 27 and 4, and 17 and 60, were followed in turn by further scores of 12, 46, 13, 29, 10 and 37 in the three Tests all won by England.

Ironically, despite these low scores, Boycott could walk out to bat at The Oval in good heart. In the previous Test, at Old Trafford, a first innings score of just 10 runs had finally taken him past Cowdrey's Test aggregate of 7,624 runs. Now only Sobers lay ahead and passing Cowdrey may have released some of the pressure on him, for Boycott proceeded to take 137 runs off the Australian attack to mark his final assault on the summit of Sobers' world record.

The Oval Test was the first occasion that a sixth Test had been played in England and, in keeping with this, showed a record-achieving status from the first day until the last. In batting, Dirk Wellham made a debut century for Australia in their second innings while Boycott, somewhat further ahead of his younger rival, came of age with his twenty-first three-figure score at Test level. For the Australians, Marsh and Yallop completed batting records by scoring respectively their 3,000th and 2,000th runs in Test cricket. No less impressive was the bowling, where the previously uncapped Terry Alderman led the way with a record 42 wickets in the series, the highest total gained by an Australian playing against England. Bob Willis and Ian Botham too were in consistent form. The former took his tally of wickets versus Australia past the 109 established by the legendary Wilfred Rhodes, while Botham claimed his 200th Test wicket. As if revelling in the challenge Dennis Lillee showed that he was still capable of withstanding comparison with any other bowler. In England's first innings he produced his best ever Test figures with an analysis of 31.4–4–89–7. Nor too was England's skipper Mike Brearley going to be left out of the limelight. He took his fiftieth catch in Test cricket and also ended his international career with an unbeaten home record as England's captain.

Boycott's century was also not without its own brand of peculiarity. In the first instance, when he reached 51 off the first delivery of the third day Boycott registered a record sixty-one half-centuries in Test cricket, (surpassing Cowdrey again!). However, although the 50 was converted into his twenty-first Test century (only one behind the England Test record of twenty-two, shared by Hammond and Cowdrey) and his 124th in all first-class cricket, it was one of Boycott's dourest efforts in any Test. It contained only *three* boundaries. Following that Boycott was leg-before to Lillee in the second innings without scoring, thus joining that select 'double' club of people who have achieved the curious distinction of making a century and nought in the same test.

That 'duck', in fact, gave Boycott an unusual 'hat-trick'. Coupled with two previous performances, one in the West Indies and one in Australia, Boycott had now made 99 and 112, 0 and 99*, and 137 and 0 in three separate Test Matches. At the least it was a rare set of figures and was probably unmatched by any other batsman in Test history. If Boycott thought himself unlucky, however, particularly in the first two instances, he could still count his blessings. At least he had two centuries to show for his labours. The Australian batsman Clem Hill, during the 1901–2 series against England, made consecutive scores of 99, 98 and 97!

When The Oval Test drew to a close, India beckoned. Boycott had now taken his Test aggregate to 7,802 runs, only 230 behind the Sobers' total of 8,032. Yet, the Australian series had not been impressive. Boycott had scored 392 runs, in twelve innings. Although his inclusion in the touring party was hardly in doubt, the figures did not lie. Boycott, now nearing forty-one years of age, was no longer the Test force of former years. The waning had set in in earnest, and if the Indian tour was a sound base from which to draw conclusions, the waning was not taking place solely on the cricket field. For some of Boycott's judgements in India, on both cricket and more human matters, were to be decidedly less than coherent to the outside observer. And very few could be blamed on the excessive heat of the Indian sun. As usual, Boycott made a rod for his own back. Only, on this occasion he overstepped the mark.

Averages for 1981 Series v Australia

Tests	I	NO	Runs	HS	Avge
6	12	0	392	137	32.66

Bowling: **Centuries:** 1
Fielding: 2   **Half-Centuries:** 1

Cumulative Test Career Averages

Tests	I	NO	Runs	HS	Avge
104	185	22	7,802	246*	47.86

Bowling: 148–45–382–7   **Centuries:** 21
Fielding: 30   **Half-Centuries:** 40

For fully two months before the tour of India began in mid-November, there was doubt that a ball would be bowled of the proposed six-Test series. The reasoning behind this was very simple. The presence of Boycott and of Northamptonshire's Geoff Cook in the England squad was not to the liking of the Indian Government because both had played first-class cricket in South Africa at varying times during their respective careers. Throughout the period of uncertainty there was feverish activity in London, Bombay and New Delhi. Finally, the protracted negotiations between the cricketing bodies of England and India, and numerous politicians, together with public pronouncements by both Boycott and Cook which voiced their disapproval of apartheid, meant that the tour was saved; however, it was a close-run affair. The issue was fraught with danger. Had the tour been abandoned it might have led to a black-white split in world cricket which could have been catastrophic for the game.

Fortunately, commonsense prevailed, the tour began on time with all of England's pre-selected players participating and the party completed the full itinerary without any discernible hitches. That, at least, was the case from an Anglo–Indian 'diplomatic' point of view. From an England cricketing stance the tour was a disaster. The series was lost, 1–0, with five Tests drawn. And when Boycott made a rapid departure for England shortly after claiming the world Test aggregate record, and then went to South Africa, it appeared to be an unseemly 'self-first and self-last' embarrassment.

The tour began on a reasonably high note. After a one-day game at Bombay's Brabourne Stadium versus a Cricket Club of India XI the tour started in earnest at Pune with a three-day fixture against an Indian Under-22 XI. Boycott immediately opened his first-class account for the winter with a century. The earlier pressures surrounding the doubtful prospects of the tour had had little, if any, effect on Boycott's play. He batted in just one innings, for four-and-a-half hours, and made 101* whilst sharing in century partnerships with Tavare (56) and then Fletcher (56*). Although not required in the second innings, when England successfully chased a target of 301 in three-and-a-half hours, Boycott had nevertheless made his mark on the tour at the earliest opportunity. Despite making such a fine start, however, Boycott's century was one of only two three-figure innings played by him on what would prove to be a foreshortened trip.

Boycott 'rested' during the next game at Nagpur, against a Board of Control President's XI, and returned to the team to take 66 and 73* off the West Zone attack at Baroda in a match that was drawn. Thus, he had raised his tour aggregate and average to 240 from three innings and one dismissal.

That third three-day fixture was also England's final preparation before the main cricketing battle began. There was still the first of three one-day internationals to play at Ahmedabad, which England won by 5 wickets, but then the team went straight into the real business of the tour by playing the first Test at Bombay. It proved to be the one decisive game of the series.

An uneven pitch, that gave a variable bounce from the start, was the unenviable prospect facing England at Bombay's Wankhede Stadium. Not surprisingly, the game did not last until much more than two hours into the fourth day. It was the fourth consecutive Test at the ground to finish in such a manner. Although Gavaskar won the toss the advantage he gained by batting was swiftly negated when his side was bowled out for 179 runs, but that low score set the tone for the remainder of the game. Yet England were given every opportunity to take charge of affairs. Following the early shock of losing Gooch at 3, Boycott and Tavare sedately wiped away 92 runs from the deficit and from a position of 95 for 1 wicket England ought to have progressed much better than they did.

Occupation of the crease was the dominant factor of the Boycott–Tavare partnership. They added their 92 runs in 59 overs but, slow as it was, the foundation had been laid on which a substantial first innings lead should have been built. England's later batsmen could not follow the example they had been shown and, after Boycott's 60 and Tavare's 56, only Fletcher (15) could reach double figures. Therefore, from 95 for 1 wicket, England tumbled to 166 all out with the artful Dilip Doshi returning figures of 29.1–12–39–5.

The consequences of squandering a possible lead quickly became apparent to England when India accumulated 227 in their second innings. By normal Test Match standards it was a modest total but it set a target of 241 runs for England to achieve victory and on such a wicket it was a very tall order indeed. Too tall, in fact; but India's final 138-run margin of victory was greater than the real difference between the sides, for, until the fourth innings of the Test, the match had always been very evenly balanced.

England were totally destroyed in their second innings. When half the side was dismissed for 42 runs the game was assured for India, and that England just reached a three-figure total was due to a last-wicket stand of 27 runs between Underwood and Willis. Whereas Doshi had tormented England initially, it was the pacemen, Kapil Dev and Madan Lal, who broke England's back latterly and each claimed 5 wickets. Madan Lal disposed of Boycott, for 3, with a delivery that kept very low and broke back viciously to trap him leg before wicket. Boycott was one more victim of the treacherous pitch but, with the Indian victory, he could take heart that it was highly unlikely that such a wicket would be made available for any of the other Tests. Batting could only get better, even if at the expense of an English defeat.

For anyone aware of the Indian outlook on Test cricket the course of the 1981–2 series was set by the result of the first Test. Gavaskar was too astute a captain, too cautious, and too proud of the possible prestige at stake, to throw away a potential winning lead in the series. One–nil would be just as good as 3–0 at the end of the series and Gavaskar's tactics in the remaining five Tests were straightforward, uncomplicated, and uncompromising. He intended to make sure that England did not win.

Before the second Test at Bangalore there was a lifeless draw at Hyderabad against South Zone. The game gave Boycott another 55 unbeaten runs. He shared in an unbroken opening stand of 186 with Gooch (119*) in the England XI's first innings but, even with the aid of three declarations, a result could not be manufactured. It was a foretaste of what would happen at Bangalore where Gavaskar was not going to take any chances at all. He had no intention of losing the series and he proved the point personally by batting for eleven hours and forty-eight minutes while scoring 172 runs for his country. It drew the immortal comment from one journalist that while Gavaskar batted, probably 100,000 Indians were born, such was the length of his innings!

England batted first and, as was their wont, Boycott and Gooch gave the innings a sound start. Eighty-eight runs were accrued in a shade over two hours, with Boycott's share being 36, until Kapil Dev found the edge of Boycott's bat and Gavaskar himself gratefully accepted the contribution in the slips. England went on to make 400 all out and, although four batsmen passed 50, none was able to achieve a century. Gavaskar could, and virtually single-handed he took India to a draw, by batting for eleven hours and forty-eight minutes to score 172 and giving India a 28-run lead. But when the tenth Indian wicket fell only four-and-three-quarter hours play was left in the match.

It meant precious little to the game that England batted for a second time but the innings was Boycott's 189th in Test cricket, thus taking him one past the world record 188 Test innings that, again, had been played by Colin Cowdrey. A century was not a viable proposition in the circumstances but Boycott did achieve the best alternative possible: another 50. On exactly that score he was bowled by a well-flighted delivery from Doshi – it was the thirtieth and last occasion he would be bowled in his Test career. England, meanwhile, sauntered to 174 for 3 wickets and the match ended as Gavaskar wanted it to end: in a draw.

Boycott's second innings at Bangalore took him to within 100 runs of Sobers' record. He now had 7,951 Test runs to his name, 81 runs adrift, and the question everybody was asking was whether Boycott would reach his goal in the third Test at New Delhi.

There was certainly no nervous dithering by Boycott as he neared the record. With hardly any fuss at all he went out to bat at Feroz Shah Kotla after Fletcher won the toss and scored 105 runs. He did not rush but nor did he waste a great deal of time. When Boycott moved from the Test centre of Bangalore to that of New Delhi he knew exactly what he had to do; he simply went out and did it. *Wisden* chronicled the event in its 1983 edition in less than enthusiastic terms: 'Of the records set, the most notable was by Boycott, who, on his way to equalling Hammond's and Cowdrey's tally of 22 Test hundreds for England, became, when 82, the most prolific of all Test batsmen, passing Sobers' 8,032 runs for West Indies (Boycott needed 190 innings to Sobers 160).'

The brackets may have the appearance of an afterthought but the comment within them was not out of context. As Sobers finished his Test career with an average of 57.78 the thirty extra innings played by Boycott represent some 1,500 runs to Sobers. It could only devalue the record, as also would Gavaskar when he took the same record from Boycott in fewer Tests and fewer innings than the Yorkshireman. It was unfortunate after Boycott had striven for so many years to reach the top of the tree, that such comparisons should be made, but it was also inevitable that statisticians would make the comparisons. For, when all was said and done, if Boycott had not opted out of Test cricket in the mid-1970s it would not have been Christmas 1981 when Boycott claimed his world Test aggregate record. It would surely have been many years earlier.

While the aggregate record was a new first for Boycott, everything else in his Test career was rapidly approaching the final stages. 'Last' was becoming the key word with regard to his actions on the Test Match stage. At New Delhi, nobody could envisage what lay ahead only days in the future, but as it was undoubtedly Boycott's penultimate Test, the final curtain was quickly coming down. The 105 he made in the third Test was Boycott's twenty-second hundred for England, and his last, and it placed him on the same mark as Cowdrey and Hammond.

Significantly perhaps, the total was four behind that achieved by Sobers during his career, seven behind Sir Donald Bradman and – still to be told – many behind Gavaskar.

During the course of his innings Boycott shared in two century partnerships, his forty-sixth and forty-seventh for England. The first, with Gooch (71), produced 132 runs for the first wicket. The Essex opener was second only to John Edrich, who partnered Boycott in six three-figure opening stands, as Boycott's most prolific partner with five such partnerships, four of them for the first wicket. Perhaps the Barber–Boycott combination of the 1960s was the most exciting pairing, because they complemented each other so well, but Gooch was a very close second to the dashing left-hander as being, if such a thing were possible, the perfect opening partner for Boycott.

When Gooch fell at New Delhi, Tavare joined forces with Boycott to add 116 runs for the second wicket and, together with his century, it proved to be Boycott's last performance of real distinction in Test cricket. The game drifted into mediocrity, with India batting but once, and in the little time that was left for England to bat a second time Boycott made 34*, or, exactly half of the total of 68 for 0 reached by close of play. The Delhi Test produced 1,031 runs for the loss of 19 wickets and it was the ultimate in boring cricket – but it had given Boycott his world record. All that remained now for him was to go to Calcutta where he could show the world what he apparently thought of his new-found status.

Ironically, Calcutta provided England with their one real chance of victory in any of the six Tests. A first innings lead was gained and only the weather and an obdurate Gavaskar prevented England from making the breakthrough. Unfortunately, shortly after the Test had finished, Boycott was winging his way back to England. Allegedly, he was ill, but the captain, Keith Fletcher, asserted that Boycott had been sent home and, because of all the behind-the-scenes friction which had taken place in India, there could be little doubt that the episode was the end of Boycott's international career.

In fact, Calcutta was the culmination of a host of Boycott anomalies that had hitherto gone unchecked. Boycott had been cossetted on the entire trip by the tour management to a degree that no man could reasonably expect. Unless that man is Geoffrey Boycott. He was given a single room (a highly unusual occurrence in touring parties). He attended very few official functions (again, somewhat unusual) and those that he did attend were not exactly graced with much 'joie de vivre'. He hardly ever socialised with his team-mates on the tour. He made tactless remarks to Indian journalists which more or less passed by without punishment.

Until, that is, the last day of the Calcutta Test. Boycott did not take his place in the field that day with the England side because of supposed illness. Instead he went off and played golf! He even asked fellow-touring members not involved in the Test if they would like to join him on the golf course. Nobody took up the offer. For each and every one of them knew that Boycott's game of golf was the biggest insult he could throw at his fellow professionals sweating it out in the heat of Calcutta's Eden Gardens.

There was to be no second 'comeback' from this sacking. If Boycott's behaviour in India had not decreed it, then his involvement in the imminent South African tour certainly would have hammered the point home. However, South Africa mattered very little in Calcutta. Nobody, other than the players involved in the enterprise, knew of any plans. No, it was purely his own behaviour in India that outlawed Boycott. Even a Boycott can only take so much rope before he hangs himself.

Thus, no more would a Test Match scorebook entry see a name penned in the following manner:

G. BOYCOTT   c. KIRMANI   b. KAPIL DEV   18
G. BOYCOTT   lbw   b. MADAN LAL   6

They were his last entries into the log book of Test Match cricket. The scores do not portray a man who, for a short while at least, had made more runs in Test history than any previous batsman. No centuries, no flourishing goodbye with the bat. Nor do the scores portray the back-door exit that Boycott made from Test cricket. Just that a comparatively little-known medium-pace bowler (outside India, that is) was the last person to claim Boycott's wicket in a Test Match. Yet, while the departure was from the rear it was, nevertheless, a Boycott-special type of finale. Not one made in a blaze of glory, but in an inferno of controversy.

Averages for 1981–82 Series v India

Tests	I	NO	Runs	HS	Avge
4	8	1	312	105	44.57

Bowling: **Centuries:** 1
Fielding: 1   **Half-Centuries:** 2

Cumulative Test Career Averages

Tests	I	NO	Runs	HS	Avge
108	193	23	8,114	246*	47.72

Bowling: 148–45–382–7   **Centuries:** 22
Fielding: 32   **Half-Centuries:** 42

N.B. The final bowling figures include both six and eight-ball overs.

14 An ignominious end

Over his whole cricketing career, Boycott always remained a complex, inscrutable player. He made mistakes but was usually forgiven by his fans. Unfortunately, however, he began to allow his personality and actions to dominate the game. By 1982, cricket had become a casualty of his ill-considered acts. For Boycott, this meant that his glorious career had come to an end in confusion and ignominy.

Put simply, the Indian tour of 1981–2 put him at the top of the highest tree in Test cricket. It also placed him, in many people's eyes, at the very lowest point. He reached his nadir and he never really recovered. For, after the tour of India took him to his final achievement there came, in unseemly haste, his involvement with the South African tour. It is difficult to separate the Indian tour from the controversy which raged about the South African one. The latter had a damaging influence on the former. The bitterness would have been bad enough if the arguments had been simply about the morality of playing in a country practising apartheid. However, the bitterness was fuelled by the way in which the tour to South Africa was organised. It was the deceit, the subterfuge, the underhand tactics and the lack of political and moral sense which left Boycott and his companions looking like 'I'm alright, Jack' mercenaries.

If the Indian authorities had had an inkling of what was afoot during the England tour of their country, they would have cancelled the tour straightaway. Instead of flouting the wishes of the Indians and upsetting so many in the cricketing fraternity, Boycott should have counted himself lucky to be allowed into India at all. The controversy surrounding previous visits to South Africa, by both himself and Geoff Cook, nearly scuppered the Indian tour before it even began. The go-ahead was not finally given until the England team were almost ready to board the plane for Bombay.

The Indians had one principal reason for allowing things to proceed which was given substantial credence by the media. It was that Boycott had written a denouncement of apartheid in a chapter of a book he had written. This in itself was fine and there was no reason to doubt its sincerity. Boycott decided to make use of this in what can only be construed as a mischievous way. During a presentation ceremony at one of the Test Matches, when the Indian Prime Minister was being introduced to the English team, Boycott suddenly produced a copy of the book and offered it to Mrs Gandhi. In terms of propaganda it was a startling display of nerve and gall, but it would probably have been acceptable if it had been a genuine attempt to demonstrate Boycott's sincerity in front of the television cameras. Even so, it was on a par with Dennis Lillee's inept request for the autograph of Her Majesty the Queen at Lord's during a similar ceremony.

His supporters would probably claim that Geoff was simply stating his case, and that he didn't support apartheid: that he honestly believed that sport and politics do not mix. Nevertheless, whilst he was publicly courting favour in India and England, he was secretly negotiating to go back to South Africa as soon as the Indian tour was over. The spirit of the Indians' wishes was being flouted and the insult was to the whole nation. England, and in particular the English side, was also treated in an unreasonable and seemingly selfish manner.

Eden Gardens, Calcutta, is an awesome place when filled to overflowing with a crowd of around 80,000 excitable fans; people who have caused some of the most fearful riots in the history of cricket. It is not a place for the faint-hearted. Even the rowdy crowds of Sydney Hill on a sultry, steamy Australian day, or at Port-of-Spain or Kingston, are nothing to compare with those of Calcutta.

The occasion has to be experienced to be believed, especially when the crowd joins in when the bowler performs his delivery. As the bowler starts his run this crowd can produce, miraculously and simultaneously, a rhythmic clapping and a low drone. There are no obvious signals and yet everyone seems to begin together. Retaining their unison throughout the bowler's run the tempo of the clapping increases and the noise rises to a crescendo. At the moment of delivery comes a tumultous climax, a full-throated roar from nearly 80,000 people: a climax almost to make the Earth move, and something very special to Test cricket. The noise alone is terrifying, but when you add to that the continual barrage of firecrackers; the throwing of oranges (a sign of affection!); or the less fair flashing of mirrors at batsmen, the atmosphere can be unnerving.

For those making their Test debuts, as Chris Old and Derek Randall once did in India, a more fiery and frightening baptism is hard to imagine. Yet what happened to the vastly experienced and hardened Geoff Boycott, playing in his 108th Test in Calcutta? What happened to the man who could have been expected to settle down, grit his teeth and help his side by showing an example? He batted twice, failed twice, and then, rather than take his place in the field, he left his team-mates to suffer the heat, dust and noise of Eden Gardens while he played golf. For that alone he surely deserved to be sent home.

Indeed, he was sent home, but a large-scale deception ensued. The story was that Boycott was ill when he flew back to England. This was put in question by later events. Keith Fletcher, the tour captain, revealed in his book *Captain's Innings* that Boycott had been dismissed at the behest of the England squad. Even before this revelation, the illness story was virtually disproved when Boycott recovered within weeks of returning from India sufficiently to leave England for South Africa. The whole affair looked like a sham.

Perhaps the worst part of Boycott's Indian behaviour was that it lent credence to all the rumours and stories which had followed him wherever he went throughout his career – stories of rudeness, self-centredness, and poor social behaviour, which had usually been seen as apocryphal, were compounded by his attitude over the Indian and South African tours. There even arose an incredible story that Boycott was alleged to have asked for the late Ken Barrington's return air ticket from the West Indies after Barrington died there on the 1980–1 tour.

The author first heard this story from a noted Indian cricketer within a week of the alleged incident occurring. Subsequently a similar tale was told to the author by players from England, Pakistan, Australia and New Zealand. The story has never been corroborated by any West Indian source and this indicates the harm that Boycott did to himself. The air ticket story, like many others, must remain a story: nonetheless, as such stories do remain, they cloud Boycott's reputation.

Boycott, in the process, became a figure of controversy, and lost all hope of becoming universally accepted either as a great personage or a great cricketer. This is truly sad. Also sad was the tearing apart of Yorkshire Cricket Club which took place in the early 1980s. It had been on the cards for over ten years and the events surrounding those turbulent times have still to be told in full. Boycott's England career was over, but the struggle for power within Yorkshire was far from over. The bitterness which was created will live on for years to come and Boycott's political and personal dealings will overshadow his real achievements. He was, after all, a first-rate cricketer and it is the intention of this book to leave readers with an impression of his cricketing achievements.

In those terms he had a superb career at international level. It touched greatness. For a while he held many Test records and was a hero in Yorkshire and England. His mistake was to forget that the game is greater than the individual and for this mistake he has paid dearly. Sunil Gavaskar soon passed Boycott and captured virtually every Test batting record in the book. Boycott's fans became divided and his once great county club was torn apart. He was left a cricketing enigma: a highly talented player, with an impressive record, who slowly destroyed what he had so dedicatedly created and became, sadly and all too soon, an unloved hero.

Statistics
Compiled by Derek Barnard

BOYCOTT'S RECORDS
to the end of the 1985 season

8,114 runs – second highest run scorer in Test cricket

---

22 hundreds – equal fifth highest century maker in Test cricket and equal first for England with Cowdrey and Hammond

---

193 Test innings – second highest number of innings ever played in Test cricket

---

246 not out – highest score in an England v India Test match

Only player to score his hundreth 100 in a Test match

When Boycott scored 107 and 80 not out for England v Australia at Trent Bridge in 1977, he became the first English player to bat on all five days of a Test match

---

He is one of the few players to have scored hundreds against all the six major Test playing countries (this excludes Sri Lanka who did not play their first Test match until 1982)

He has scored hundreds on all six Test match grounds in England

---

In scoring 99 and 112 for England v West Indies at Port-of-Spain in 1973–4, he became the first batsman in Test cricket to score 99 and a century in the same Test match

---

He was awarded the OBE in the 1980 Birthday Honours List

HIGHEST TEST RUN AGGREGATES
correct to end of January 1986

Runs	Name	Tests	I	NO	HS	100	Avge
9,192	S. M. Gavaskar	112	195	16	236*	32	51.35
8,114	G. Boycott	108	193	23	246*	22	47.73
8,032	G. S. Sobers	93	160	21	365*	26	57.78
7,624	M. C. Cowdrey	114	188	15	182	22	44.06
7,515	C. H. Lloyd	110	175	14	242*	19	46.67
7,249	W. R. Hammond	85	140	16	336*	22	58.45
7,110	G. S. Chappell	87	151	19	247*	24	53.86
6,996	D. G. Bradman	52	80	10	334	29	99.94
6,971	L. Hutton	79	138	15	364	19	56.67

BOYCOTT'S RECORD IN TEST CRICKET

Tests	I	NO	Runs	HS	100	Avge
108	193	23	8,114	246*	22	47.73

BOYCOTT'S DISMISSALS IN TEST CRICKET

Innings	193
Bowled	31
Lbw	27
Run out	7
Stumped	2
Caught and bowled	5
Caught	98
Not out	23

BOYCOTT'S INNINGS AGAINST EACH COUNTRY IN TEST CRICKET

Country	Tests	I	NO	HS	Runs	100	Avge
Australia	38	71	9	191	2,945	7	47.50
India	13	22	3	246*	1,084	4	57.05
New Zealand	15	25	1	131	916	2	38.17
Pakistan	6	10	3	121*	591	3	84.43
South Africa	7	12	2	117	373	1	37.30
West Indies	29	53	5	128	2,205	5	45.94
Totals	**108**	**193**	**23**	**246***	**8,114**	**22**	**47.73**

Highest Score   246 not out, England v India first Test match at Headingley, Leeds 1967.

BOYCOTT'S BOWLING IN TEST MATCHES

Season	Opponents	Overs	Maidens	Runs	Wickets	Avge
1964	Australia	1	0	3	0	—
1964–5	South Africa	61	16	157	5	31.40
1965	South Africa	26	10	60	0	—
1965–6	Australia	23	4	89	2	44.50
1965–6	New Zealand	12	6	30	0	—
1970–1	Australia	1	0	7	0	—
1977–8	Pakistan	3	0	4	0	—
1978–9	Australia	1	0	6	0	—
1979	India	7	3	8	0	—
1980	West Indies	7	2	11	0	—
1980–1	West Indies	3	2	5	0	—
1981	Australia	3	2	2	0	—
Totals		**148**	**45**	**382**	**7**	**54.57**

Best Bowling   3–47 against South Africa third Test match at Cape Town, 1964–5.

BOYCOTT'S INNINGS IN TEST CRICKET

Season	Scores/ how out	Opponents	Venue	Test number
1964	48 ct	Australia	Trent Bridge	1
	38 ct, 4 ct	Australia	Headingley	2
	58 b	Australia	Old Trafford	3
	30 b, 113 ct	Australia	The Oval	4
1965–5	73 lbw	South Africa	Durban	5
	4 ct	South Africa	Johannesburg	6
	15 ct, 1 no	South Africa	Cape Town	7
	5 ct, 76 no	South Africa	Johannesburg	8
	117 ct, 7 ct	South Africa	Port Elizabeth	9
1965	23 ct, 44 no	New Zealand	Edgbaston	10
	14 ct, 76 lbw	New Zealand	Lord's	11
1965	31 ct, 28 ct-b	South Africa	Lord's	12
	0 ct, 16 b	South Africa	Trent Bridge	13
1965–6	45 b, 63 no	Australia	Brisbane	14
	51 b, 5 no	Australia	Melbourne	15
	84 ct-b	Australia	Sydney	16
	22 ct, 12 lbw	Australia	Adelaide	17
	17 ct, 1 lbw	Australia	Melbourne	18
	4 ct, 4 ro	New Zealand	Christchurch	19
	5 b	New Zealand	Dunedin	20
1966	60 ct, 25 ct	West Indies	Lord's	21
	0 lbw, 71 ct	West Indies	Trent Bridge	22
	12 ct, 14 ct	West Indies	Headingley	23
	4 b	West Indies	The Oval	24
1967	246 no	India	Headingley	25
	25 st, 6 b	India	Edgbaston	26
	15 b, 1 no	Pakistan	Trent Bridge	27
1967–8	68 lbw	West Indies	Port-of-Spain	28
	17 b, 0 b	West Indies	Kingston	29
	90 lbw	West Indies	Bridgetown	30

Season	Scores/ how out	Opponents	Venue	Test number
	62 ct, 80 no	**West Indies**	Port-of-Spain	31
	116 ct, 30 b	**West Indies**	Georgetown	32
1968	35 ct, 11 ct	**Australia**	Old Trafford	33
	49 ct	**Australia**	Lord's	34
	36 lbw, 31 ct	**Australia**	Edgbaston	35
1969	128 lbw, 1 no	**West Indies**	The Oval	36
	23 ct, 106 ct	**West Indies**	Lord's	37
	12 lbw, 0 ct	**West Indies**	Headingley	38
	0 ct, 47 ct	**New Zealand**	Lord's	39
	0 b	**New Zealand**	Trent Bridge	40
	46 b, 8 b	**New Zealand**	The Oval	41
1970–1	37 ct, 16 ct	**Australia**	Brisbane	42
	70 ct, 50 st	**Australia**	Perth	43
	77 ct, 142 no	**Australia**	Sydney	44
	12 ct, 76 no	**Australia**	Melbourne	45
	58 ro, 119 no	**Australia**	Adelaide	46
1971	121 no	**Pakistan**	Lord's	47
	112 ct, 13 ct	**Pakistan**	Headingley	48
	3 ct, 33 ct	**India**	Lord's	49
1972	8 ct, 47 lbw	**Australia**	Old Trafford	50
	11 b, 6 b	**Australia**	Lord's	51
1973	51 lbw, 1 ro	**New Zealand**	Trent Bridge	52
	61 ct, 92 ct-b	**New Zealand**	Lord's	53
	115 ct	**New Zealand**	Headingley	54
	97 ct, 30 ct-b	**West Indies**	The Oval	55
	56 no	**West Indies**	Edgbaston	56
	4 ct, 15 ct	**West Indies**	Lord's	57
1973–4	6 ct, 93 ct	**West Indies**	Port-of-Spain	58
	68 ct, 5 ct	**West Indies**	Kingston	59
	10 ct, 13 ct	**West Indies**	Bridgetown	60
	15 b	**West Indies**	Georgetown	61
	99 ct, 112 b	**West Indies**	Port-of-Spain	62
1974	10 lbw, 6 ct	**India**	Old Trafford	63

Season	Scores/ how out	Opponents	Venue	Test number
1977	107 ct, 80 no	**Australia**	Trent Bridge	64
	191 ct	**Australia**	Headingley	65
	39 ct, 25 no	**Australia**	The Oval	66
1977–8	63 b	**Pakistan**	Lahore	67
	79 ro, 100 no	**Pakistan**	Hyderabad	68
	31 b, 56 ct	**Pakistan**	Karachi	69
	77 ct, 1 b	**New Zealand**	Wellington	70
	8 lbw, 26 ro	**New Zealand**	Christchurch	71
	54 ct	**New Zealand**	Auckland	72
1978	131 ct-b	**New Zealand**	Trent Bridge	73
	24 ct, 4 b	**New Zealand**	Lord's	74
1978–9	13 ct, 16 ro	**Australia**	Brisbane	75
	77 lbw, 23 lbw	**Australia**	Perth	76
	1 b, 38 lbw	**Australia**	Melbourne	77
	8 ct, 0 lbw	**Australia**	Sydney	78
	6 ct, 49 ct	**Australia**	Adelaide	79
	19 ct, 13 ct	**Australia**	Sydney	80
1979	155 lbw	**India**	Edgbaston	81
	32 ct	**India**	Lord's	82
	31 ct	**India**	Headingley	83
	35 lbw, 125 b	**India**	The Oval	84
1979–80	0 lbw, 99 no	**Australia**	Perth	85
	8 b, 18 ct	**Australia**	Sydney	86
	44 ct, 7 b	**Australia**	Melbourne	87
	22 ct, 43 no	**India**	Bombay	88
1980	36 ct, 75 b	**West Indies**	Trent Bridge	89
	8 ct, 49 no	**West Indies**	Lord's	90
	5 ct, 86 lbw	**West Indies**	Old Trafford	91
	53 ro, 5 ct	**West Indies**	The Oval	92
	4 ct, 47 ct	**West Indies**	Headingley	93
	62 ct, 128 no	**Australia**	Lord's	94
1980–1	30 ct, 70 ct	**West Indies**	Port-of-Spain	95
	0 b, 1 ct	**West Indies**	Bridgetown	96
	38 ct, 104 no	**West Indies**	Antigua	97
	40 ct, 12 ct	**West Indies**	Kingston	98

Season	Scores/ how out	Opponents	Venue	Test number
1981	27 ct, 4 ct	**Australia**	Trent Bridge	99
	17 ct, 60 ct	**Australia**	Lord's	100
	12 b, 46 lbw	**Australia**	Headingley	101
	13 ct, 29 ct	**Australia**	Edgbaston	102
	10 ct, 37 lbw	**Australia**	Old Trafford	103
	137 ct, 0 lbw	**Australia**	The Oval	104
1981–2	60 ct, 3 lbw	**India**	Bombay	105
	36 ct, 50 b	**India**	Bangalore	106
	105 ct, 34 no	**India**	Delhi	107
	18 ct, 6 lbw	**India**	Calcutta	108

Abbreviations:
b = bowled
ct = caught
ct-b = caught and bowled
lbw = leg before wicket
st = stumped
ro = run out
no = not out

CENTURY IN EACH INNINGS OF A FIRST CLASS MATCH

103 and 105	Yorkshire v Nottinghamshire	Sheffield 1966
160* and 116	England v The Rest	Worcester 1974
163 and 141*	Yorkshire v Nottinghamshire	Bradford 1983

BOYCOTT'S INNINGS
SEASON BY SEASON – FIRST CLASS MATCHES
to end of 1985 English season

Season	Matches	I	NO	Runs	HS	100	Avge
1962	5	9	2	150	47	—	21.43
1963	28	43	7	1,628	165*	3	45.22
1964	27	44	4	2,110	177	6	52.75
1964–5	15	25	5	1,135	193*	4	56.75
1965	26	44	3	1,447	95	—	35.29
1965–6	13	21	2	784	156	1	41.26
1966	28	50	3	1,854	164	6	39.45
1967	24	40	4	1,910	246*	4	53.06
1967–8	11	16	2	1,154	243	4	82.43
1968	20	30	7	1,487	180*	7	64.65
1969	23	39	6	1,283	128	3	38.88
1969–70	1	2	0	7	7	—	3.50
1970	25	42	5	2,051	260*	4	55.43
1970–1	12	22	6	1,535	173	6	95.94
1971	21	30	5	2,503	233	13	100.12
1971–2	1	2	0	148	107	1	74.00
1972	13	22	5	1,230	204*	6	72.35
1973	18	30	6	1,527	141*	5	63.62
1973–4	10	16	3	960	261*	3	73.85
1974	21	36	6	1,783	160*	6	59.43
1975	19	34	8	1,915	201*	6	73.65
1976	12	24	5	1,288	207*	5	67.79
1977	20	30	5	1,701	191	7	68.04
1977–8	13	20	3	867	123*	3	51.00
1978	16	25	1	1,233	131	6	51.38
1978–9	12	23	3	533	90*	—	26.65
1979	15	20	5	1,538	175*	6	102.53
1979–80	8	15	4	599	110	2	54.45
1980	17	28	4	1,264	154*	3	52.67
1980–1	9	17	2	818	104*	1	54.53
1981	16	28	2	1,009	137	3	38.81
1981–2	12	21	5	905	105	2	56.56
1982	21	37	6	1,913	159	6	61.70
1983	23	40	5	1,941	214*	7	55.45
1984	20	35	10	1,567	153*	4	62.68
1985	21	34	12	1,657	184	6	75.31
Totals	596	994	161	47,434	261*	149	56.94

*Not out

BOYCOTT'S BOWLING
SEASON BY SEASON – FIRST CLASS MATCHES
to end of 1985 English season

Season	Overs	Maidens	Runs	Wickets	Avge
1963	2	0	20	0	—
1964	17	4	55	0	—
1964–5	94	24	262	8	32.75
1965	72.1	30	134	4	33.50
1965–6	84	25	285	4	71.25
1966	12	5	25	0	—
1967	22	3	77	2	38.50
1967–8	13.3	5	27	2	13.50
1968	3	1	10	0	—
1969	4.3	2	13	0	—
1969–70	3	1	5	0	—
1970–1	4.4	0	31	1	31.00
1973–4	9	1	33	1	33.00
1977	10	4	16	1	16.00
1977–8	4	0	5	0	—
1978	12	6	13	0	—
1978–9	3	0	11	0	—
1979	52.2	23	92	9	10.22
1979–80	4	0	19	0	—
1980	51	15	82	4	20.50
1980–1	3	2	5	0	—
1981	14	7	20	0	—
1982	57.2	13	120	8	15.00
1983	23	10	45	1	45.00
1984	11	0	25	0	—
1985	10	2	29	0	—
Totals	**595.3**	**183**	**1,459**	**45**	**32.42**

Best Bowling   14.2 overs   9 maidens   14 runs   4 wickets
for Yorkshire v Lancashire at Leeds, 1979.

BOYCOTT'S CENTURIES IN FIRST CLASS CRICKET

Year	Score	For	Against	Venue	Number
1963	145	Yorkshire	Lancashire	Sheffield	1
	113	Yorkshire	Lancashire	Manchester	2
	165*	Yorkshire	Leicestershire	Scarborough	3
1964	151	Yorkshire	Middlesex	Leeds	4
	131	Yorkshire	Lancashire	Manchester	5
	151*	Yorkshire	Leicestershire	Leicester	6
	122	Yorkshire	Australia	Bradford	7
	113	England	Australia	The Oval	8
	177	Yorkshire	Gloucestershire	Bristol	9
	193*	MCC	Eastern Province	Port Elizabeth	10
	106	MCC	Western Province	Cape Town	11
1965	114	MCC	Invitation XI	Cape Town	12
	117	England	South Africa	Port Elizabeth	13
1966	156	MCC	Combined XI	Hobart	14
	123	Yorkshire	MCC	Lord's	15
	136*	Yorkshire	Warwickshire	Birmingham	16
	164	Yorkshire	Sussex	Hove	17
	103	Yorkshire	Nottinghamshire	Sheffield	18
	105	Yorkshire	Nottinghamshire	Sheffield	19
	131	TN Pearce's XI	West Indies	Scarborough	20
1967	102	Yorkshire·	Glamorgan	Harrogate	21
	246*	England	India	Leeds	22
	220*	Yorkshire	Northamptonshire	Sheffield	23
	128	Yorkshire	Pakistan	Leeds	24
	135	MCC	President's XI	Bridgetown	25
1968	165	MCC	Leeward Islands	Antigua	26
	243	MCC	Barbados	Bridgetown	27
	116	England	West Indies	Georgetown	28
	100	Yorkshire	Sussex	Bradford	29
	132	Yorkshire	Leicestershire	Leicester	30
	180*	Yorkshire	Warwickshire	Middlesbrough	31
	125	Yorkshire	Gloucestershire	Bristol	32
	114*	Yorkshire	Leicestershire	Sheffield	33
	102*	Yorkshire	MCC	Scarborough	34
	115*	England XI	Rest of the World XI	Scarborough	35

Year	Score	For	Against	Venue	Number
1969	128	England	West Indies	Manchester	36
	106	England	West Indies	Lord's	37
	105*	Yorkshire	Somerset	Leeds	38
1970	148	Yorkshire	Kent	Sheffield	39
	260*	Yorkshire	Essex	Colchester	40
	157	England	Rest of the World XI	The Oval	41
	147*	England XI	England U25 XI	Scarborough	42
	173	MCC	South Australia	Adelaide	43
	129*	MCC	New South Wales	Sydney	44
	124	MCC	Queensland	Brisbane	45
	126	MCC	Western Australia	Perth	46
	142*	England	Australia	Sydney	47
	119*	England	Australia	Adelaide	48
1971	110	Yorkshire	Warwickshire	Middlesbrough	49
	112*	Yorkshire	Middlesex	Leeds	50
	169	Yorkshire	Nottinghamshire	Leeds	51
	121*	England	Pakistan	Lord's	52
	233	Yorkshire	Essex	Colchester	53
	182*	Yorkshire	Middlesex	Lord's	54
	112	England	Pakistan	Leeds	55
	133	Yorkshire	Derbyshire	Scarborough	56
	169	Yorkshire	Lancashire	Sheffield	57
	151	Yorkshire	Leicestershire	Bradford	58
	111	Yorkshire	Hampshire	Bournemouth	59
	138*	Yorkshire	Warwickshire	Birmingham	60
	124*	Yorkshire	Northamptonshire	Harrogate	61
1972	107	Northern Transvaal	Rhodesia	Pretoria	62
	122*	Yorkshire	Somerset	Taunton	63
	105	Yorkshire	Lancashire	Leeds	64
	100	Yorkshire	Nottinghamshire	Worksop	65
	204*	Yorkshire	Leicestershire	Leicester	66
	121	Yorkshire	Essex	Chelmsford	67
	105	Yorkshire	Hampshire	Southampton	68
1973	141*	Yorkshire	Cambridge University	Cambridge	69
	101	Yorkshire	Lancashire	Manchester	70
	114	D. Robin's XI	West Indies	Eastbourne	71
	115	England	New Zealand	Leeds	72
	129	Yorkshire	Nottinghamshire	Bradford	73

Year	Score	For	Against	Venue	Number
1974	261*	England	West Indies Board of Control President's XI	Bridgetown	74
	133*	England	Guyana	Georgetown	75
	122	England	West Indies	Port-of-Spain	76
	140	Yorkshire	Cambridge University	Cambridge	77
	160*	England	The Rest	Worcester	78
	116	England	The Rest	Worcester	79
	149*	Yorkshire	Derbyshire	Sheffield	80
	117	Yorkshire	Sussex	Leeds	81
	142*	Yorkshire	Surrey	Bradford	82
1975	152*	Yorkshire	Worcestershire	Worcester	83
	141	Yorkshire	Gloucestershire	Bristol	84
	173*	Yorkshire	Middlesex	Scarborough	85
	139	Yorkshire	Nottinghamshire	Sheffield	86
	201	Yorkshire	Middlesex	Lord's	87
	105*	Yorkshire	Lancashire	Leeds	88
1976	161	Yorkshire	Gloucestershire	Leeds	89
	207*	Yorkshire	Cambridge University	Cambridge	90
	141	Yorkshire	Nottinghamshire	Bradford	91
	156*	Yorkshire	Glamorgan	Middlesbrough	92
	103*	Yorkshire	Lancashire	Manchester	93
1977	139*	Yorkshire	Somerset	Harrogate	94
	103	Yorkshire	Australia	Scarborough	95
	117	Yorkshire	Middlesex	Lord's	96
	154	Yorkshire	Nottinghamshire	Nottingham	97
	107	England	Australia	Nottingham	98
	104	Yorkshire	Warwickshire	Birmingham	99
	191	England	Australia	Leeds	100
	123*	England	United XI	Faisalabad	101
	115*	England	NW Frontier Gvnr's XI	Peshawar	102
1978	100*	England	Pakistan	Hyderabad	103
	115	Yorkshire	Warwickshire	Birmingham	104
	113	Yorkshire	Northamptonshire	Northampton	105
	103	Yorkshire	New Zealand	Leeds	106
	118	Yorkshire	Glamorgan	Sheffield	107
	131	England	New Zealand	Nottingham	108
	129	Yorkshire	Nottinghamshire	Scarborough	109
1979	151*	Yorkshire	Derbyshire	Leeds	110
	130*	Yorkshire	Somerset	Harrogate	111

Year	Score	For	Against	Venue	Number
	167	Yorkshire	Derbyshire	Chesterfield	112
	155	England	India	Birmingham	113
	175*	Yorkshire	Nottinghamshire	Worksop	114
	125	England	India	The Oval	115
	101*	England	Tasmania	Hobart	116
	110	England	South Australia	Adelaide	117
1980	135	Yorkshire	Lancashire	Manchester	118
	128*	England	Australia	Lord's	119
	154*	Yorkshire	Derbyshire	Scarborough	120
1981	104*	England	West Indies	Antigua	121
	124	Yorkshire	Nottinghamshire	Bradford	122
	122*	Yorkshire	Derbyshire	Derby	123
	137	England	Australia	The Oval	124
	101*	England	India U22 XI	Pune	125
	105	England	India	Delhi	126
1982	138	Yorkshire	Northamptonshire	Northampton	127
	134	Yorkshire	Glamorgan	Leeds	128
	159	Yorkshire	Worcestershire	Sheffield	129
	152*	Yorkshire	Warwickshire	Leeds	130
	122*	Yorkshire	Sussex	Scarborough	131
	129	Yorkshire	Somerset	Weston-Super-Mare	132
1983	112	Yorkshire	Derbyshire	Sheffield	133
	101	Yorkshire	Kent	Sheffield	134
	214*	Yorkshire	Nottinghamshire	Worksop	135
	140*	Yorkshire	Gloucestershire	Cheltenham	136
	163	Yorkshire	Nottinghamshire	Bradford	137
	141*	Yorkshire	Nottinghamshire	Bradford	138
	169*	Yorkshire	Derbyshire	Chesterfield	139
1984	104	Yorkshire	Kent	Tunbridge Wells	140
	153*	Yorkshire	Derbyshire	Harrogate	141
	126*	Yorkshire	Gloucestershire	Bradford	142
	101	Yorkshire	Glamorgan	Cardiff	143
1985	114*	Yorkshire	Somerset	Leeds	144
	115	Yorkshire	Hampshire	Middlesbrough	145
	105*	Yorkshire	Worcestershire	Harrogate	146
	184	Yorkshire	Worcestershire	Worcester	147
	103*	Yorkshire	Warwickshire	Birmingham	148
	125*	Yorkshire	Nottinghamshire	Scarborough	149

Index

Abdul Qadir 94
Alderman, T.M. 118
Ali, S. Abid 69, 84
Allen, D.A. 25, 35
Amiss, D.L. 73, 74, 76, 77,
  79, 80, 81, 82
Arnold, G.G. 74, 75
Athey, C.W.J. 112

Bacchus, S.F.A.F. 109
  Barber, R.W. 25, 26, 29,
  30, 34, 35, 36, 37, 39, 40,
  52, 88, 123
Barlow, E.J. 24
Barrington, K.F. 25, 26, 28,
  29, 31, 34, 36, 43, 46, 49,
  108, 113, 127
Bartlett, G.A. 37
Bedi, B.S. 44
Bedser, A.V. 72, 76, 84
Birkenshaw, J. 83
Bland, K.C. 25, 26
Bolus, J.B. 16, 17
Booth, B.C. 20
Botham, I.T. 87, 88, 96,
  104, 106, 107, 108, 109,
  116, 117, 118
Botten, J.T. 24
Boyce, K.D. 77, 79, 80, 83
Bradman, Sir D.G. 108,
  112, 123
Bracewell, B.P. 98, 99
Brearley, J.M. 86, 88, 89,
  90, 91, 94, 103, 104, 106,
  117, 118
Bright, R.J. 87
Brown, D.J. 25, 35, 37, 38,
  46, 47
Burge, P.J. 21, 22, 34
Burgess, M.G. 74
Burke, S.F. 26
Butcher, B.F. 41, 46, 47,
  48, 58

Camacho, G.S. 46, 47
Carew, G.M. 56
Cartwright, T.W. 25

Chandrasekhar, B.S. 44
Chappell, G.S. 90, 91, 105
Chappell, I.M. 52, 53, 64
Chauhan, C.P.S. 104, 105
Close, D.B. 32, 41, 43
Collinge, R.O. 74, 96
Congdon, B.E. 74
Connolly, A.N. 63
Cook, G. 119, 125
Corling, G.E. 20, 21, 22
Cowdrey, M.C. 22, 36, 48,
  49, 53, 54, 55, 63, 64, 72,
  108, 116, 117
Cowper, R.M. 36, 53, 54
Croft, C.E.H. 111
Crookes, N.S. 24
Cunis, R.S. 37

Daniel, W.W. 87
Davis, C.A. 57
Denness, M.H. 82, 83, 84
Dexter, E.R. 29
D'Oliveira, B.L. 41, 43, 49,
  52, 58, 64, 65
Doshi, D. 120, 121, 122
Dowe, V.G. 80
Dowling, G.T. 44
D'Souza, A. 16
Dumbrill, R. 24, 31
Dymock, G. 106

Edmonds, P.H. 104
Edrich, J.H. 19, 21, 30, 33,
  34, 35, 36, 39, 47, 48, 49,
  52, 53, 54, 56, 57, 58, 62,
  63, 64, 65, 83, 123
Elizabeth II, Queen 87
Engineer, F.M. 44, 84

Fagg, A.E. 76
Fletcher, K.W.R. 63, 74, 75,
  82, 83, 120, 122, 123, 126
Fredericks, R.C. 57, 79, 80, 83

Gandhi, Mrs I 126
Garner, J. 109
Gavaskar, S.M. 13, 69, 70,

  83, 103, 104, 105, 120,
  121, 122, 123, 127
Ghavri, K.D. 104
Gibbs, L.R. 40, 48, 49, 76,
  79, 80, 82, 83
Gleeson, J.W. 53, 63
Goddard, T.L. 25, 26
Gooch, G.A. 37, 98, 103,
  106, 107, 109, 112, 114,
  117, 120, 121, 123
Gower, D.I. 103, 106, 117
Graveney, T.W. 40, 43, 46,
  48, 49, 54, 56, 57
Grieg, A.W. 82, 83, 88, 89
Griffin, G.M. 38
Griffith, C.C. 38, 40, 41,
  46, 47
Greenidge, C.G. 111
Grout, A.T.W. 19, 20, 22
Guha, S. 44

Hadlee, D.R. 73
Hadlee, R.J. 96, 97, 98
Hall, W.W. 46, 47
Hammond, W.R. 43, 53, 54,
  62, 108, 114, 118, 122
Hampshire, J.H. 57, 58, 100
Hardstaff, J.(Jun) 89
Haroon Rashid, 94
Hawke, N.J.N. 20, 22, 23,
  35, 36
Haynes, D.L. 110
Hendrick, M. 92
Hendriks, J.L. 57
Higgs, K. 37
Hill, C. 118
Hobbs, Sir J.B. 96
Hobbs, R.N.S. 46
Holding, M.A. 98, 110, 114,
  115
Holford, D.A.J. 40
Howarth, G.P. 97
Howarth, H.J. 74
Hughes, K.J. 112
Hutton, Sir L. 14, 16, 89,
  103, 108, 112
Hutton, R.A. 68

Illingworth, R. 16, 57, 58, 63, 64, 65, 66, 68, 74, 75, 83, 100
Imran Khan, 95
Imtiaz Ahmed 16
Inshan Ali 83
Iqbal Qasim 93, 95
Ishmael, S. 82

Jackman, R.D. 113
Jaisimha, M.L. 88
Jarman, B.N. 52
Javed Miandad 94
Jenner, T.J. 63
Johnson, C. 100
Johnson, P.D. 87
Jones, I.J. 49
Julien, B.D. 79, 81

Kallicharran, A.I. 76, 77, 80, 83, 90
Kanhai, R.B. 41, 46, 48, 76, 77, 80, 81, 82, 83
Kapil Dev 103, 104, 121, 124
Kentish, E.S.M. 76
Kirmani, S.M.H. 124
Knight, B.R. 38
Knott, A.P.E. 48, 49, 52, 55, 58, 77, 80, 81, 88, 89, 90
Kunderan, B.K. 43, 44

Lawrence, J. 15
Lawry, W.M. 36, 53, 54, 63, 64, 65
Leadbeater, B. 87
Lewis, A.R. 73
Lillee, D.K. 46, 72, 106, 112, 115, 117, 118, 126
Lloyd, C.H. 57, 80, 82, 83
Lock, G.A.R. 48
Love, J. 86, 89
Luckhurst, B.W. 62, 63, 65, 68

Macaulay, M.J. 24
Mackay-Coghill, M. 24
McCosker, R.M. 88, 89, 97
Mckenzie, G.D. 20, 21, 22, 23, 34, 35, 36, 52, 53, 80
McKinnon, A.H. 31
Madan Lal 121, 124
Mallett, A.A. 64
Malone, M.F. 86
Marsh, R.W. 90, 92, 117, 118
Massie, R.A.L. 72

Melville, J.E. 16
Milburn, C. 39, 40, 41, 53
Miller, G. 88
Mohol, S.N. 44
Motz, R.C. 29, 38
Mudassar Nazar 93, 94
Murray, D.L. 47, 76, 82, 83, 109
Mushtar Mohammad, 95

Nurse, S.M. 41, 46

Old, C.M. 81, 89, 90, 101, 102, 112, 115, 126
O'Neill, N.C. 20

Packer, K. 94, 105
Parfitt, P.H. 22, 26, 30, 31, 37, 58
Parkinson, M. 101
Parks, J.M. 25, 31, 34, 40
Partridge, J.T. 25
Pascoe, L.S. 88, 112
Pataudi, M.A.K. 43
Pearce, T.N. 42
Philpott, P.I. 35
Pocock, P.I. 48, 49, 52, 81
Pollard, V. 37, 44, 74
Pollock, P.M. 24, 30
Pollock, R.G. 25, 26, 30
Prasanna, E.A.S. 44
Price, J.S.E. 25

Radley, C.T. 98
Randall, D.W. 37, 88, 89, 92, 103, 126
Redpath, I.R. 23, 52, 53, 54, 66
Rhodes, W. 118
Roberts, A.M.E. 110, 114
Robins, D.H. 77
Roope, G.R.J. 90
Rose, B.C. 96
Rowe, L.G. 82, 83
Russell, W.E. 34, 39

Sang Hue 82
Sharpe, P.J. 57, 58
Sheahan, A.P. 52, 53
Shepherd, J.N. 57, 58
Shillingford, G.C. 58
Sidebottom, A. 87
Sikander Bakht 94
Simpsom, R.B. 20, 21, 22, 23, 36

Smedley, M.J. 87
Smith, M.J.K. 16, 24, 26, 31, 34
Snow, J.A. 31, 52, 54, 57, 62, 63, 64, 69
Sobers, Sir G.S. 40, 41, 47, 48, 49, 57, 58, 80, 81, 82, 83, 92, 93, 99, 108, 116, 117, 118, 122, 123
Solkar, E.D. 84
Speight, A. 14
Spofforth, F.R. 114
Stott, W.B. 17
Subramanya, V. 44
Surti, R.F. 44
Sutcliffe, H. 15
Sutcliffe, W.H.H. 15

Tavare, C.J. 109, 120, 123
Taylor, B.R. 73
Taylor, K. 32
Taylor, R.W. 16, 106, 107
Thomson, J.R. 46, 89, 90, 115
Thomson, N.I. 25
Titmus, F.J. 19, 20, 25, 31, 34, 35, 48
Trueman, F.S. 22, 23

Underwood, D.L. 76, 80, 81, 121

Veivers, T.R. 34
Vengsarkar, D.B. 104
Venkataraghavan, S. 44, 69
Vishwanath, G.R. 104
Vivian, H.G. 29

Wadsworth, K.J. 74
Walker, M.H.N. 86, 89, 92
Walters, K.D. 52, 53
Wasim Bari, 94
Welham, D.M. 118
Willey, P. 110
Willis, R.G.D. 71, 72, 94, 97, 101, 106, 109, 110, 113, 118
Wood, G.M. 112
Woodcock, J. 84
Woolmer, R.A. 88, 109, 110, 117
Worthington, T.S. 43

Yallop, G.M. 118

Zaheer Abbas 95

144